NEIGHBORS IN MOB:
2 BOOKS IN 1
THE MAFIA HISTORY IN PENNSYLVANIA AND NEW JERSEY

MAFIA LIBRARY

© **Copyright 2024 - All rights reserved.**

The content contained within this book may not be reproduced, duplicated or transmitted without direct written permission from the author or the publisher.

Under no circumstances will any blame or legal responsibility be held against the publisher, or author, for any damages, reparation, or monetary loss due to the information contained within this book, either directly or indirectly.

Legal Notice:

This book is copyright protected. It is only for personal use. You cannot amend, distribute, sell, use, quote or paraphrase any part, or the content within this book, without the consent of the author or publisher.

Disclaimer Notice:

Please note the information contained within this document is for educational and entertainment purposes only. All effort has been executed to present accurate, up to date, reliable, complete information. No warranties of any kind are declared or implied. Readers acknowledge that the author is not engaged in the rendering of legal, financial, medical or professional advice. The content within this book has been derived from various sources. Please consult a licensed professional before attempting any techniques outlined in this book.

By reading this document, the reader agrees that under no circumstances is the author responsible for any losses, direct or indirect, that are incurred as a result of the use of the information contained within this document, including, but not limited to, errors, omissions, or inaccuracies.

TABLE OF CONTENTS

The Bruno-Scarfo Mafia Crime Family

Introduction 1

Chapter 1 : Early History of the Philly Mob 3
- Origins 3
- Salvatore Sabella and Early Criminal Undertakings 6
- The First Philadelphia Mafia War 9
- The Expansion of Joseph 'Joe Bruno' Dovi 12

Chapter 2 : Powerful Connections: Vito Genovese and the Five Families of New York 15
- Vito Genovese and the Five Families 16
- Joseph Ida 18
- The Philly Mob and the Commission 20
- The 1957 Apalachin Meeting 22

Chapter 3 : 'The Gentle Don': Angelo Bruno 25
- The Bruno Crime Family 25
- The Gambino Connection 28
- Pressure Begins to Build 30
- Bruno's Murder 32

Chapter 4 : A Struggle for Power: The Second Philadelphia Mafia War 35

    Power Vacuum 36

    Nicodemo Scarfo Takes Power 37

    Scarfo's Reshuffle 39

    No Tribute 41

Chapter 5 : The Gambler's Fallacy: Atlantic City 45

    Crime and Atlantic City 46

    Fall, Then Rise 48

    Scarfo's Stomping Ground 51

Chapter 6 : Ruthless and Paranoid: Nicodemo 'Little Nicky' Scarfo 55

    The Mob Under Scarfo 56

    The Mind of a Mafia Boss 58

    Scarfo's Downfall 61

    Ruling Behind Bars 64

Chapter 7 : The War to End All Wars: John Stanfa and the Third Philadelphia Mafia War 67

    The Appointment of Stanfa 68

    A Divide in the Family 69

    Bugged and Jailed 73

    'Front Boss' Natale 75

Chapter 8 : The Politics of Crime: Ralph Natale and Joseph Merlino 79

    The Puppet Boss 79

    Merlino's Notoriety 82

    King Rat 83

Chapter 9 : To Flee a Sinking Ship: Rats 87

    From Cop to Bouncer to Soldier: Ron Previte 88

    Childhood Mobster: Phil 'Crazy Phil' Leonetti 91

    Headshot Survivor: John Veasey 93

    Scarfo's Hitman: Nicholas 'Nicky Crow' Caramandi 99

Chapter 10 : The 'Modern' Philly Mob: Joseph Ligambi and the Return of Merlino 103

    Joseph Ligambi 104

    A Period of Stability 106

    Merlino's Return 109

    The Philly Mob Today 112

Conclusion 115

References 117

Introduction 125

The Decavalcante Mafia Crime Family

Chapter 1 : Family History.. 129
    Family Origins: The Elizabeth and Newark Families 131

    Bootlegging and Early Criminal Activities............................. 134

    Trouble in Newark 135

    The First Bosses 138

    Rise of "The Count": Simone DeCavalcante....................... 145

Chapter 2 : DeCavalcante.. 147
    Sam The Plumber.. 147

    Riggi's Way: John "The Eagle" Riggi 151

    John D'Amato: The Original Gay Mobster......................... 154

    Jake Amari: The Real-Life Jackie Aprile.............................. 157

Chapter 3 : Maintaining the Family's Reputation 161
    The Inferiority Complex 162

    The Media Blitz 163

    The Bungled Heist.. 166

    The Consequences of Discord 168

    Riggi's Extended Sentence... 169

    The Old Man.. 170

    Guarraci Steps In 171

    Trouble in Las Vegas... 173

    Charles "Big Ears" Majuri 176

Chapter 4 : Jersey Boys 181
Italian-American Communities in New Jersey 181
The First Wave of Immigration 181
Elizabeth and Newark 183
The Ribera Club and Other Hangouts 186
The Laws of the Streets 190
Organized Crime in New Jersey 191

Chapter 5 : Five Families Connections 195
Flying Under the Flag of the Gambinos 196
The Genovese Dilemma 201
Stango's Dealings With the Lucchese and Colombo Families 204
Rotondo's Bonanno Family Encounter 205
The King of Wall Street 207

Chapter 6 : The Philadelphia Connection 211
Sam the Plumber and Angelo Bruno 211
Don't Shoot the Messenger 214
Atlantic City 217

Chapter 7 : The Family Today 221
Cocaine 221
On the Waterfront 222
Dealing and Distribution 223
Prostitution 225
Waste Management and Illegal Dumping 228
The Construction Racket 230

Chapter 8 : Rats 235

    Big-Mouthed Rat, Anthony Rotondo 235

    Wannabe Wiseguy Rat, Ralph "Ralphie" Guarino 238

    Rat From the Suburbs, Vincent "Vinny Ocean" Palermo 242

    Witness Protection 245

Chapter 9 : The Real Sopranos 249

Conclusion 253

References 255

THE BRUNO-SCARFO MAFIA CRIME FAMILY

INTRODUCTION

Mafia is a process, not a thing. Mafia is a form of clan; cooperation to which its individual members pledge lifelong loyalty. Friendship, connections, family ties, trust, loyalty, obedience: this was the glue that held us together. –Joseph Bonanno

Organized crime, or more specifically, the Mafia, is an entity that has permeated society, catching fascination on multiple levels. One is through popular fictionalized content, including Francis Ford Coppola's *The Godfather* trilogy of films and, more recently, HBO's television series *The Sopranos* and *Boardwalk Empire*. Their accounts of self-made gangsters rising through the ranks, gaining wealth and power, through usually illicit means, against the backdrop of 20th century America have captivated audiences from their initial release until the present day. The above quote from Joseph Bonanno, who was Boss of the Bonanno Crime Family from 1931 to 1968, provides another perspective: one of cooperation, loyalty, and family, where the core tenants of the organization as a tightly knit unit truly encapsulate what it is to be a mafia family (Margaritoff, 2022). These films and shows do, of course, explore the Mafia, the key players within, and the activities organized crime are involved with, and Bonanno's quote provides an insider's perspective on the importance of loyalty and family within the Mafia. That being said, it is important that we do not become disconnected from one critical fact: that organized crime is a very real entity that both had and continues to have a stranglehold of influence on the society that we live in. The true nature of organized crime is then perhaps better understood as not solely encompassed by its representation in either the media or the quote from Bonanno, but in both, and, in intertwining the two, we come to see a more focused and accurate picture of organized crime as a whole.

Out of the numerous mafia organizations that arose and operated from the early 20th century and onward, there is one that tore a swathe of power, influence, and opulence from its inception to the modern day: the Philadelphia Crime Organization. Known by many names and colloquially as the Philly Mob, this organization carved out its territory initially in Philadelphia, then quickly moved its operations into other states, such as New Jersey and beyond. The Philly Mob's history is rife with bloody internal conflicts, shifting power structures, and aggressive expansion, cementing the organization in the annals of organized crime history as well as creating a sphere of influence that, within their territories, can be felt even today. From its beginnings as separate Italian-American street gangs, through to the rise and fall of various Bosses like Angelo Bruno, Nicodemo Scarfo, and Ralph Natale, to its position as a credible power within modern-day society under Joseph Merlino, this book will take you on a journey through the history of the Philly Mob, the plethora of dealings and activities it associated itself with, and the trail of carnage it left in its wake.

It seems then appropriate to kickstart this exploration with a newspaper headline, published in 1995 by The New York Times, that provides a perfect example of the nature and influence of the Philly Mob, as well as the lengths it would go to showcase its power: "Brother of Mob Turncoat is Gunned Down" (Raab, 1995).

CHAPTER 1
EARLY HISTORY OF THE PHILLY MOB

As with many powerful and intricate crime organizations, the Philly Mob did not spring into existence as developed and influential as it came to be later. The organization's inception is a widely contested discussion point, with historians and journalists finding various sources that suggest multiple beginnings of the organization that would come to be known as the Philly Mob. Here, we will explore these points, journeying through the exploits and eventual amalgamation of the plethora of street gangs in Philadelphia. It would be this amalgamation that would be the beginnings of the Philly Mob that we still feel the influence of in the modern day.

Origins

Shrouded in mystery and conflicting reports, the inception of an organized criminal outfit, or a Mafia, in Philadelphia sprung from the gangs that already existed and operated throughout the United States at the tail end of the 19th century. A slew of Sicilian and Italian immigrants had begun to settle in the United States at this time, and it is purported that "Americans [first] became acquainted with the word, 'Mafia' when the major wave of immigration of Sicilians…had settled in New Orleans in the 1860s" (Morello, 1999, p. 7). This organized criminal activity, while seen to be happening in other areas of the United States, such as New Orleans, Chicago, and New York, cannot be accurately linked to Philadelphia and its surrounding areas at this time in history. It seems that, towards the end of the 19th century, Philadelphia as a city had only "a secondary role in organized crime" (Morello, 1999, p. 13), with Secret Service agents who were attempting to stamp out the criminal activity at the time, finding only vague links with persons or groups in Philadelphia when arresting more extensive criminal networks in places like New York City. As Celeste Morello writes, "Identifying the Mafia was a difficult obstacle to overcome. Evidently, there was no proof of a Mafia in Philadelphia at that time" (Morello, 1999, pp. 13-14).

Of course, due to the very nature of organized criminal activity, just the fact that there was no proof of Mafia activity in Philadelphia does not mean that it did not exist. There are sources that suggest that "Mafiosi and Black Hand extortionists existed in the Philadelphia area from about the turn of the 20th century, possibly earlier" (Hunt, 2023). To clarify, mafioso refers to an official member of either the Sicilian or Italian-American Mafia, as well as any other Italian criminal organization. Black Hand refers to a type of Italian extortion racket brought to the United States with the Sicilian and Italian immigrants, operations of which were firmly rooted in numerous major American cities at the beginning of the 20th century, such as New York City, Chicago, and indeed Philadelphia. It is important to note at this point that Black Hand activity in Philadelphia, and indeed in the United States as a whole, was not so much an organized institution of individuals who dealt in criminal activities but more, so a method of extortion used by

Italian mobsters. That being said, it is clear that, by the beginning of the 20th century, Black Hand activity is documented to have been occurring in Philadelphia, "overshadow[ing] all other 'Italian' ethnic crime by its overt symbols - the inked handprint and letters sent with demands" (Morello, 1999, p. 19). Indeed, Nicola Gentile (a Sicilian mafioso during this early period) published memoirs claiming, "that he was inducted into a crime family in Philadelphia around 1907", although this information is "confined to a footnote" and Gentile mentioned "nothing else about the organization or the city" (Hunt, 2023). Within the various criminal organizations operating in Philadelphia at this time, there were "deep factional divisions" (Hunt, 2023). While all were predominantly of Italian heritage, criminal individuals tended to drift towards groups that shared their specific regional identities. These groups included the more traditional Mafia organization of the western Sicilians, along with street gangs made up of Calabrians and eastern Sicilians. This by no means indicates a structured criminal organization present in Philadelphia, however, with "a significant division between Sicilian and Calabrian factions [lingering] in the crime family" even after consolidation (Hunt, 2023).

From this, we can see that, at this time, the existence of a singular and independent Philadelphia crime family is difficult to pinpoint and cohesively prove beyond a shadow of a doubt. On the other hand, we can see that criminal activities were indeed occurring within the city of Philadelphia and its surrounding areas, some of which can be at least somewhat linked to operations run by more extensive crime networks in other American cities. It seems clear that while it is evident that "Philadelphia indeed was a Mafia site of activity" at this time, it is quite unclear as to whether this was an independent entity in and of itself or was "an appendage of a New York Family" (Morello, 1999, p. 26). Regardless of the vague and mysterious beginnings of what would come to be known as the Philly Mob, the turn of the 20th century would see the apparent spattering of street gangs and criminal rackets coalesce into an independent and cohesive criminal organization, an organization headed by one particular man: Salvatore Sabella.

Salvatore Sabella and Early Criminal Undertakings

Salvatore Sabella began his life in 1891, born to parents John and Rosa in Castellammare del Golfo, Sicily. It is interesting to note that numerous individuals who went on to become organized crime leaders in the United States came from this Sicilian town, including Sabella, Joseph Bonnano, and Stefano Magaddino, with Morello (1999) describing the area as "the birthplace of the Mafia" (p.41). Throughout Sabella's formative years, there is one instance that sent the young Sicilian on a journey that found him heading a crime organization of his own and, quite ironically, may have indeed prepared him for this calling. At fourteen years of age, Sabella found himself working as an apprentice to a butcher (a career path he would return to after his retirement from the Philly Mob in 1931). The butcher young Sabella worked under tended towards violent outbursts, the brunt of which seemed to fall upon Sabella. One fateful day in 1905, having had enough of the butcher's abuse, Sabella retaliated, killing him. Years later, in 1908, Sabella was charged for the butcher's murder and subsequently arrested, spending his three-year prison sentence in Milan, Italy. During his incarceration, it is thought that Sabella joined the Sicilian Mafia, promptly leaving for the United States after his release. Arriving in Brooklyn, New York, in 1912, Sabella quickly joined in with organized criminal activities, training to one day take a leadership role within the organization. That role came when, in 1919, Sabella was sent to Philadelphia to create a Sicilian criminal organization to operate there. With that, Salvatore Sabella joined the various street gangs and criminal organizations that operated in Philadelphia, becoming the first recognizable Boss of the Philly Mob.

The term 'recognizable' to describe Sabella's rise to power is used very specifically here, as it is predominantly clear that there were other leaders prior to Sabella. These leaders did not use the familiar titles and ran criminal activities that were not as organized as they were to become when Sabella took over. However, criminal enterprise in Philadelphia still existed prior to Sabella's arrival, and that enterprise required some vestige of hierarchy to operate effectively. As one of Sabella's soldiers stated, "There were many Bosses here before Salvatore Sabella" (Morello, 1999, p. 39). In fact, "to further [confuse] matters for historians," some of these early Bosses seemingly used the title of *rappresentante*, indicated to be "a sort of liaison or family ambassador" (Hunt, 2023). This role of *rappresentante* can be seen as a progenitor of sorts to the more formal designation of Boss that would come to be used later, with the *rapprensentante* acting as "a single regional spokesman for a fragmented underworld with multiple Bosses" (Hunt, 2023). With this in mind, it was these pockets of criminal enterprises that Sabella had to work with when he arrived in Philadelphia. Sabella set the beginnings of the Philly Mob on busying themselves with various criminal activities. He led them to begin bootlegging: the smuggling of alcoholic beverages forbidden by law. Practically all of Sabella's reign as Boss was during Prohibition-era America. They began using extortion: the usually violent practice of gaining benefit through coercion. This was accompanied by loansharking: the practice of offering unlawful loans with extremely high-interest rates and usually violent consequences for failure to pay. They also began running illegal gambling rings: casino gambling was not made legal in the wider United States until much later in the century. There were factions of the criminal underworld in Philadelphia that did not appreciate Sabella's hostile takeover of their turf, arguably the most notable of which were the Zanghi brothers.

The Zanghi brothers, Anthony 'Muskie' Zanghi and Joseph Zanghi ran a local gang that feuded with Sabella's Philly Mob. While not acting wholly separate from the Philly Mob, the Zanghi brothers were known to be rebellious, seemingly preferring their own control as opposed to operating under the jurisdiction of Sabella. Having caused Sabella much trouble and difficulty, including being a suspect in the attempted murder of top lieutenant and future Boss John Avena, Sabella, along with Avena and others, decided to "send a message loud and clear: the streets of South Philadelphia were theirs - and would remain theirs" (Finkel, 2014). The message would come in 1927 when a drive-by shooting orchestrated by Sabella killed Joseph Zanghi and injured Anthony Zanghi. This hit would have consequences for Sabella, as the surviving Zanghi brother "broke the [gangster] code of silence" (Finkel, 2014), going straight to the police. Though Sabella was ultimately acquitted, the investigation led investigators to find Sabella to have entered the United States without proper documentation, ending with Sabella being deported back to Sicily later that year, with Avena taking over as acting Boss in Sabella's absence. The later years of Sabella's reign over the Philly Mob primarily took place outside of Philadelphia. He returned to the United States in 1929 to participate in the New York Castellammarese War. The conflict ended in 1931 with a victory for Sabella's side, and he returned to Philadelphia to resume control of the Philly Mob. This return, however, was short-lived. In the same year, Sabella was arrested once again for assault and battery with a motor vehicle. Shortly after, Sabella retired from organized crime, passing the leadership of the Philly Mob over to acting Boss John Avena. The reasoning for Sabella's retirement was and has remained unknown, and he was reported to have lived his life as a butcher in Norristown, Pennsylvania, until his death from natural causes in 1962. With Sabella retired and a criminal organization to run, Avena took his place as the new Boss. However, he was not without his challengers.

The First Philadelphia Mafia War

As we will see time and time again during this exploration, the rank of Boss is a position that, when left empty, creates a bloody and drawn-out power struggle that ends with one victor sitting atop the carnage. Being no exception to this rule, the space at the head of the Philly Mob left after Sabella's departure was fought over in a five-year conflict known as the First Philadelphia Mafia War, with new Boss and alleged designated choice of his predecessor John Avena and another of Sabella's top lieutenants during his reign, Joseph 'Joe Bruno' Dovi heading the warring factions. Both men hailed from the Sicilian eastern region of Messina, with Avena born in 1893 and Dovi four years earlier in 1889. Another similarity between the two mobsters was that the majority of individuals taken into the fold of the Philly Mob had Western Sicilian heritage, with other regions of Sicily "generally regarded as outside the Mafia tradition" (Hunt, 2023). The 'made men' of the Philly Mob (in other words, the official and fully initiated members of the Mafia) at this time, despite usually requiring the individual to be Italian or of Italian descent, tended to be of this specific and traditional heritage. Regardless of this tradition, however, the main players in the First Philadelphia Mafia War were Avena and Dovi, and an ensuing battle for power was about to begin.

Avena had been close with Sabella, having been indicted along with him and others in the drive-by shooting of the Zanghi brothers, and was purportedly Sabella's choice to succeed him as Boss. Known as *Nasone* in Italian, translated to English as 'Big Nose,' Avena had been a staple in the Philadelphia criminal underworld since his arrival in the city in 1908. According to Hunt, Avena "reportedly moved into organized crime first as a Black Hand extortionist and later as a bootlegger and gambling racketeer" (Hunt, 2023). With the aforementioned indictment along with Sabella in 1927, Avena's standing within the Philly Mob seems to have been both respected and influential. Dovi, on the other hand, is harder to place in correlation to his activities within the organization before his grab for power, with his role within the Philly Mob during this time being "unclear" (Hunt, 2021). Born Giuseppe Dovi, but known more by his nickname 'Joe Bruno,' Dovi arrived in the United States as a teenager and moved and began operating in Philadelphia after a short stint in western New York state. While the details of Dovi's activities at this time are hazy, he was *consigliere* to Sabella, and he likely commanded a certain amount of power and influence within the Philly Mob, hence his challenge to Avena for the title of Boss.

The five-year conflict of the First Philadelphia Mafia War was bookended by the activities of a gang of criminal brothers: the Lanzetta brothers. The six brothers (Leo, Pius, Ignatius, Hugo, Lucian, and Teofilo) operated in South Philadelphia, involving themselves in various criminal activities. Their operation brought them into conflict with the Philly Mob, a conflict that went back to the days of Sabella's reign as Boss. Sabella was suspected of having been involved in the murder of Leo Lanzetta in 1925, and this grudge lasted into the reign of Avena. While the civil war between Avena and Dovi raged from 1931 to 1936, the "rebellious faction" led by the Lanzetti brothers "arose in the Philadelphia area" (Hunt, 2021). Under Avena, the Philly Mob had created a partnership with the Jewish 69th Street Mob, cementing them as leaders in the illegal gambling enterprise of Philadelphia. This power move brought the Philly Mob into direct conflict with the Lanzetta brothers, who also had a significant stake in the illegal gambling trade, worsening the already bubbling feud and "may ultimately have cost Avena his life" (Hunt, 2023). In 1936, the third attempt on Avena's life was successful, as Avena was shot to death in a brutal drive-by shooting. The Lanzetta brothers were key suspects in the murder, which effectively ended the First Philadelphia Mafia War and left the position of Boss of the Philly Mob open for the taking, a position filled without hesitation by Dovi.

The Expansion of Joseph 'Joe Bruno' Dovi

Dovi officially became the Boss of the Philly Mob in 1936, wasting no time in consolidating and expanding the Philly Mob's operations in Philadelphia and beyond. Dovi had good connections with other powerful and influential crime organizations within the United States, including the Chicago Outfit (run by the infamous gangster Al 'Scarface' Capone) and the Five Families of New York (a formation of five major organized crime families operating out of New York City). These connections, along with a more aggressive and expansionist ideology from Dovi, allowed the Philly Mob to spread its influence across the Greater Philadelphia Area, Atlantic City, and even into southern New Jersey. The Philly Mob's activities and enterprises remained largely similar under Dovi, with the majority of the organization's income being from selling narcotics, along with the more familiar loansharking, extortion, and illegal gambling. Additionally, Dovi's tenure as Boss saw the settling of the long feud with the Lanzetta brothers, further solidifying the Philly Mob's hold over Philadelphia. This expansion also had another, more organic effect. With the ever-growing expansion of the Philly Mob came the interest of and connection with even more crime organizations, specifically the Gambino and Genovese crime families. Members of the Five Families of New York, these connections continued to grow throughout, and indeed long after, Dovi's reign as Boss.

Dovi was different from his predecessors. While Salvatore Sabella and John Avena held a similar philosophy, one of being 'hands-on' so to speak, in the affairs of the organization, Dovi held a diametric view, preferring to "[keep] his distance from the Philadelphia underworld" (Hunt, 2023). He ruled over the Philly Mob from various locations, none of which were in Philadelphia. Firstly, he dealt with his responsibilities as Boss from his residence in Bucks County, which was around 40 miles northeast of the city. Then, he relocated to Trenton, which, while technically closer, is in New Jersey. Both Sabella and Avena had resided in the city of Philadelphia itself. While this geographical point is interesting to make, it seems to have had no negative effect on Dovi's ability to effectively lead the Philly Mob to further prosperity throughout the late 1930s and well into the 1940s. In 1946, Dovi died of natural causes in a New York hospital, again leaving the Philly Mob without a Boss. However, the landscape of organized crime in the United States was changing, with the eyes of powerful individuals falling on the Philly Mob and its growing influence. They saw an opportunity and were most definitely going to seize it.

CHAPTER 2
POWERFUL CONNECTIONS: VITO GENOVESE AND THE FIVE FAMILIES OF NEW YORK

As we have seen in the previous chapter, the importance of connection within the world of organized crime cannot be understated. Those one knows and has a strong relationship with can be invaluable allies, especially in a cutthroat world where one's standing can rise and fall as quickly as the breeze changes. That being said, the state of the Philly Mob during the lead-up and at the death of Joseph Dovi was one of opportunity and expansion, a spreading fire fueled by some of the most powerful and influential criminal entities operating in the United States at the time. The Five Families of New York, specifically the Genovese Family, and even more specifically Vito Genovese, were the powers-that-be that drove the Philly Mob further up the hierarchy of criminal organizations. Here, we will explore the broader context of the organized criminal entities that surrounded the Philly Mob, the Philly Mob's connection to said entities, and the power shift that occurred in the criminal underworld of the United States, with the Philly Mob as the focus, during the 1940s up to the late 1950s.

Vito Genovese and the Five Families

To call Vito Genovese an important individual in the context of the Mafia and organized crime in the United States would only be scratching the surface. That being said, there is very little space here to truly delve into the intricacies of Genovese himself and the wider Genovese crime family, who were one of the major players in the Five Families of New York. What is prevalent here is the connection that Genovese and his family had to the rising organization, the Philly Mob. After the Castellammarese War in 1931, the same conflict that former Philly Mob Boss Salvatore Sabella took part in, Genovese and Luciano were integral to reorganizing the crime syndicates of the United States, officializing the Five Families and creating the Commission. In 1956, Genovese went from underboss to Boss of what would later be named the Genovese crime family when an assassination attempt, concocted by Genovese, on previous Boss Frank Costello failed to kill him, but did succeed in "[pushing] Costello into retirement" (*Notable Names: Vito Genovese*, 2015). Now head of a powerful crime family and having seen the gains made by the Philly Mob started by Joseph Dovi, Genovese made moves to exert control over the burgeoning organization from Philadelphia. So exceptional was the influence Genovese had on the Philly Mob in fact that, as the Philly Mob's growth continued into southern New Jersey and Atlantic City, many viewed it as simply as a Genovese faction as opposed to an independent crime organization.

In the same vein as Genovese, the other crime families of New York also looked towards the Philly Mob with eyes full of opportunity, wanting a cut of their profitable activities. The Five Families of New

York had been set up in the aftermath of the Castellammarese War and was composed of the most powerful organized crime syndicates operating in the United States. The families that comprise the group are now known as the Bonnano, Colombo, Genovese, Gambino, and Lucchese families. At the organization's inception, each family was intended to report to Salvatore Maranzano, the victor of the Castellammarese War, who gave himself the title of *'capo dei capi'* or 'boss of all bosses.' This self-given, and some would argue vain, title drew ire, however, and Marazano was assassinated, the role of 'boss of all bosses' being replaced by the Commission. As we can see from this brief explanation of the Five Families, the Philly Mob is not mentioned as part of the conglomerate, further reinforcing the idea that the Philly Mob was not regarded as a top power in the Mafia families at this time. As previously mentioned, the Genovese family had a large influence over the Philly Mob, as did connections grow with Carlo Gambino, a high-ranking member of the Gambino crime family and ally of future Philly Mob Boss Angelo Bruno. Suffice it to say that these connections with other crime families both helped and hindered the Philly Mob: helped by allowing the organization to grow its own power and influence across a large area of the United States and hindered by devaluing the Philly Mob's position as a wholly independent criminal organization, demoting it to simply another appendage of the monster that was the Five Families of New York.

Joseph Ida

Giuseppe 'Joseph' Ida was born in Fiumara, Italy, in 1890. The year 1919 saw Ida come to the United States, settling in the south of Philadelphia, where it seems he quickly found himself enveloped in the criminal activities of the Philly Mob. Purportedly, "there was always something to say about Joe Ida that was disconcerting. He was around for a while and supposedly was involved in everything from interstate prostitution to killings to gambling and narcotics" (Morello, 2005, p.58). At some point, Ida was introduced to then Boss Salvatore Sabella, his underboss John Avena, and *consigliere* Joseph 'Joe Bruno' Dovi. While it is complete conjecture to suggest that Ida met all three at the same time, Ida seemingly had, in quick succession, met all three of his predecessors. In fact, in the aftermath of the 1927 drive-by shooting of the Zanghi brothers, he was charged along with Sabella and Avena for his participation in the crime, although none were ultimately convicted. When Dovi took over as Boss after Avena's murder, he chose Ida as his underboss. After Dovi's death in 1946, the newly formed Commission appointed Ida as his successor. From Dovi, Ida inherited a Philly Mob that was steadily growing its power while also dealing with the grasping hands of other larger criminal organizations.

Ida was the Philly Mob's first non-Silician Boss and, like his predecessor Dovi, "lived some distance from Philadelphia during his term as Boss," his residence being "considerably closer to New York City than to Philadelphia" (Hunt, 2023). Again, just like his predecessor, this fact did not hinder Ida's ability to grow the Philly Mob's power and influence as, under his watchful eye, "the crime family reportedly expanded" (Hunt, 2023). Ida drove out the Jewish mobsters operating in Philly Mob territory, effectively ending the presence of the Jewish Mob in Philadelphia and southern New Jersey. It was also under the reign of Ida that "illegal narcotics were tied publicly to the Philadelphia-South Jersey Family as never before" (Morello, 2005, p. 71). The trafficking of narcotics, while, of course, a very risky business, saw massive returns in profit for those that involved themselves and were successful. As the Philly Mob continued to grow in South Jersey and Atlantic City, along with this push in the sale of narcotics, Ida felt the invasive hands of the Genovese family, which had been ever-present, grip further around his organization. The Genovese family sought to influence the comings and goings of numerous families, and as previously covered in this chapter, the growth of the Philly Mob was of particular interest to underboss Vito Genovese. This influence would stay for the moment, but under Ida, the Philly Mob continued to make their mark on the criminal underworld, pushing ever closer to their standing as an independent power in their own right.

At this point, instead of discussing the end of Ida's reign as Boss (a part of the Philly Mob's history that is intrinsically linked to an event that will be discussed later in this chapter), let us discuss the individual that took power (albeit briefly) directly after, acting as the bridge between Ida's reign and the reign of Philly Mob heavyweight Angelo Bruno: Antonio Pollina. From Sicily, Pollina had been active in the Philly Mob since at least 1927, with arrests for murder, assault, and concealed weapons, and was yet another one of the Philly Mob members to be indicted for the drive-by shooting of the Zanghi brothers. In late 1958, Pollina was thrust into the position of Boss after Ida departed from the United States. While seemingly more than happy to take the position (being the leader of an organized crime family does have its perks, after all), "the year 1959 would be unforgettable for Antonio Domenico Pollina" (Morello, 2005, p. 78). Serving his tenure as Boss from within the city of Philadelphia, Pollina's "proximity to the Philly rackets did not help his popularity with the crime family membership," and the Commission began to notice "deep division in the organization" (Hunt, 2023). This lack of recognition (the Commission reportedly designated Pollina as 'interim Boss' until order could be restored to the family) was made worse by Pollina, who began plotting to murder Angelo Bruno, a well-respected Mafia member and Pollina's self-decided rival. Why Pollina decided this is unclear; however, Bruno later commented that "it was just a manifestation of jealousy on Pollina's part" (Morello, 2005, p. 78). Due to the respect Bruno commanded, as well as Pollina's own underboss revealing his murder plans, Pollino was stripped of his power and forced to step down. The Commission even authorized Bruno to murder Pollina, although this did not happen, with Pollina living out his life "as a dishonored Mafioso" until his death at 101 years of age in 1993. Leaving with the words of Pollina himself towards the end of his life, "God wants me to live so I can suffer" (Morello, 2005, p. 99).

The Philly Mob and the Commission

As we have seen, the Commission sprung into existence at the outset of the Castellammarese War in 1931. Its creation was in aid of overseeing all Mafia activity in the United States, to create a third party to mediate and solve disputes between families, to unify the collection of crime families and networks operating in the same territories and protect the interests of all criminal organizations under one overarching jurisdiction. After the debacle that was Maranzano and his 'boss of all bosses' moniker, those in power felt that the Commission was a less provocative and more efficient way of presiding over the criminal families of the United States. At its inception, the Commission was composed of a ruling committee on which sat each Boss of the Five Families of New York as well as the Bosses of the Chicago Outfit. The Commission's responsibilities manifested in many ways, such as "approving new members, controlling relations between [the Commission] and the Sicilian Mafia, [and] formally recognizing new bosses" (Petepiece, 2018, p. 18). While this all sounds quite formal, let us not forget that the Commission oversaw all Mafia enterprises in the United States. These responsibilities sometimes required a darker and more brutal nature, "taking steps to maintain order between families including the use of murder and creating an atmosphere of fear concerning the Commission to ensure obedience" (Petepiece, 2018, p. 18). The Commission was not without its downfalls, with plots by members to assassinate other members being rather commonplace (the most well-known of these instances being Joe Bonnano's failed coup in 1963) as well as constant police attention and scrutiny, eventually leading to the Mafia Commission Trial in 1985. These future events aside, the Commission was, at this time, the new power in the criminal underworld, a power that the various crime families had to work with in order to continue their enterprises.

This is the landscape that Ida's Philly Mob found itself rising through the ranks around the mid-to-late 1950s. As has been made clear by both the setup of the Commission and the actions and influences of the larger crime families whose Bosses were committee members of said Commission, the Philly Mob was not at the table, so to speak, when it came to holding any power or sway within the ruling organization. This fact, however, was very rapidly approaching a complete turnaround. After a 1956 Commission meeting, the Philly Mob, along with the Detroit Partnership led by Joseph Zerilli and the Buffalo crime family headed by Stefano Magaddino, were inducted into the Commission, their leaders being given places on the committee. For the Philly Mob, this move onto the Commission cemented its position as a functioning and influential criminal organization in and of itself, one that acted independently from any other. This was a pivotal moment in the history of the Philly Mob, a moment where it garnered its reputation as a genuine power in the criminal underworld, paving the way for a slew of infamous Bosses that came in the preceding decades, as well as its familiar title of the Bruno-Scarfo Mafia crime family. This is, however, jumping the gun somewhat, as Ida still firmly held control over the Philly Mob in 1956. That is, of course, until this firm grip began to loosen, the catalyst of which was the events of the Apalachin Meeting in 1957.

The 1957 Apalachin Meeting

The 1957 Apalachin Meeting was a summit meeting of the American Mafia hosted at the home of mobster Joseph 'Joe the Barber' Barbara in Apalachin, New York. On the agenda for the meeting were allegedly topics such as narcotics trafficking, gambling, loansharking, and the dividing up of recently murdered mobster Albert Anastasia's illegal enterprises amongst the other criminal networks. The meeting also served another purpose. It gave Vito Genovese, who had just taken control of the Genovese crime family (named the Luciano crime family before his takeover) from Frank Costello, a way to legitimize his power by calling on the leaders of all crime families and criminal networks operating at the time to attend. Barbara's house was chosen as the location for the meeting as it was "200 miles northwest of New York City and the prying eyes of police" (Dunn, 2021). Over 100 Mafioso are reported to have attended, all "[barreling] down the highways to rural New York in sleek, brand-new Cadillacs" (Dunn, 2021). This detail is imperative, as it was this that tipped off the authorities as to what was occurring. New York State police detective Ed Croswell "saw dozens of gleaming Cadillacs parked next to the only paved stretch of backroad leading to Barbara's house" and immediately "knew something was up" (Dunn, 2021). With roadblocks set up, the police quickly raided the meeting. In an attempt to flee, many gangsters fled into the surrounding woods of Barbara's estate, clad in expensive jewelry and suits. Purportedly, locals in the area stated that, even months after the event, "they were still picking hundred-dollar bills out of the leaves in the woods around the house" (Dunn, 2021). In total, the authorities arrested and indicted 62 criminal Bosses, although the charges brought before them did not stick. However, an important outcome of the raid on the Apalachin Meeting was the shedding of light on the criminal underworld, an entity the existence of which authorities had long refused to acknowledge.

Coming back into relation with the Philly Mob, we can now pick back up with Joseph Ida, who, along with his underboss Dominick 'Big Dom' Oliveto, were of the many mobsters that attended the Apalachin Meeting and also were arrested when it was raided by law enforcement, Ida himself being identified and indicted on a drug trafficking charge. As Morello (2005) puts it, "Apalachin was Ida's downfall, a lasting defeat, a betrayal by so-called friends in a fellowship that he thought was more than a family" (pp. 73-74). Ida was taking no chances, fleeing back to Sicily in late 1958. This left Antonio Pollina, whom we discussed earlier, in the position of acting Boss in Ida's absence. Some sources do claim Ida did not flee, remaining in the United States. These, however, are sparse, to say the least, and it is widely held that Ida "settled in Fiumara and, within a couple of years, renounced the U.S. citizenship he acquired through naturalization" (Hunt, 2023). Ida would never return to the United States. Despite those in the Philly Mob calling him "the Boss who fled," Ida remained in Fiumara, spending his time hunting, with law enforcement's interest in him slowly fading to nothing. (Morello, 2005, p. 77). After the departure of Ida and the removal of Pollina by the Commission, eyes turned to who would next take the leadership of the Philly Mob. The Commission, who now had a say in the matter, had an idea of whom they wanted running the Philadelphia organization. That individual was Angelo Bruno.

CHAPTER 3
'THE GENTLE DON': ANGELO BRUNO

Up to this point in the exploration, we have witnessed the creation of the Philly Mob, its expansion from pockets of warring criminal factions to a unified Mafia family, and its inclusion amongst the big players of organized criminal entities in the United States. We have seen this burgeoning criminal organization led by five Bosses: Sabella, Avena, Dovi, Ida, and Pollina, each taking the reins of the Philly Mob in their own unique ways and all experiencing successes and failures. Now, we find ourselves on the precipice of Angelo Bruno's tenure as Boss of the Philly Mob. Portrayed on film in *Legend* and by actor Harvey Keitel in Martin Scorsese's *The Irishman*, Bruno, known as 'The Gentle Don,' saw out a 21-year reign over Philadelphia's criminal underworld; a reign so impactful that the family he ran became referred to as the Bruno crime family. In this chapter, we will explore this reign, discussing Bruno's style of leadership, his connections and relationships with other prominent mobsters, the events that led up to his eventual downfall, and just how brutal that downfall was.

The Bruno Crime Family

Moving to the United States as a child, Sicilian-born Angelo Annaloro (Bruno later dropped that last name and began using his paternal grandmother's maiden name) was the son of a grocery store owner in Feltonville, Philadelphia, a store in which the young Bruno would "often [pick] up shifts" to help out his father (McKennett, 2019). He attended school briefly but dropped out after only a few years to open his own grocery store in Passyunk Square. Bruno's first of many arrests came in 1927 for reckless driving, and he "got involved in the Philadelphia Mob at a young age," his sponsor in the criminal organization taking the form of reputable criminal Michael Maggio. Bruno's falling in with the Philly Mob was the catalyst of his name change, reportedly doing so "as a homage to Philadelphia mobster 'Joe Bruno' Dovi" (McKennett, 2019). The rap sheet Bruno would accrue during the period before his ascension to Boss reads as familiar as any who were involved in organized crime, with arrests for illegal gambling, receiving stolen property, and firearms violations among the charges. Bruno also came to own numerous legitimate businesses, all of which did business outside of Philadelphia, such as an extermination company in New Jersey, an aluminum products company in Florida, and a share in the Plaza Hotel in Cuba, running them throughout his tenure as Boss of the Philly Mob. In context to his personal life, Bruno had married in 1931, having two children with his wife Assunta 'Sue' Bruno, with Bruno being "extremely dedicated to his family" (McKennett, 2019). Bruno, his wife, and children lived in South Philadelphia, and this was the residence from which Bruno "commanded the underworld" during his time as Boss (Hunt, 2023).

Technically, Bruno succeeded Joseph Ida as the Boss of the Philly Mob in 1959. Although Antonio Pollina had indeed taken over from Ida before this, his role was simply seen as 'interim' by all but Pollina himself. From the brief exploration of Pollina in the previous chapter, one can see that Pollina had a grudge against Bruno. After hearing of Pollina's plans to murder him, Bruno used his connections to the Commission to have Pollina deposed. Far from just being the Commission's top choice for the rank of Boss, they even gave him their blessing to assassinate Pollina. Bruno declined the latter and, by doing so, "displayed the mercy that characterized his reign by instead ordering Pollina into retirement" (Hunt, 2023). Under Bruno, the Philly Mob's power and influence grew exponentially, with Bruno expanding operations in Atlantic City, which had come to be known as Philly Mob turf. Law enforcement discovered in 1963 that Bruno and Phillip Testa had been making numerous trips to Atlantic City from Philadelphia, the fact being insinuated into both reinforcing the idea that Philly Mob operations were increasing rapidly in the area and that Bruno collaborated closely with Testa. Bruno also oversaw the Philly Mob's gambling syndicate, preferring more traditional Mafia activities such as loansharking, numbers games, and infiltrating legitimate businesses. Despite several arrests, Bruno avoided any substantial prison time, most likely due to his "connections with powerful politicians and power brokers" (McKennett, 2019). The longest prison time Bruno served came in 1970 for refusing to testify at a hearing regarding organized crime, for which he received nearly three years. Unlike his predecessors and fellow crime Bosses, "Bruno approached his criminal acts with the mindset of a businessman, which meant less gang violence and more profit" (McKennett, 2019). Bruno hoped that, by taking this path, he had "a chance to transform the mob into a more legitimate business" (McKennett, 2019).

Of course, one does not attain the nickname 'The Gentle Don' for nothing. Starting with the mercy shown to Pollina, Bruno preferred to seek peaceful solutions to issues and conflicts as opposed to violent ones. He had a "disdain for unnecessary violence" that came across explicitly in his style of leadership (McKennett, 2019). For example, he forbade his men from involving themselves in the sale of narcotics, fearing both the long prison sentences that came with them and the amount of attention from law enforcement that those activities would bring. That being said, violence was still the go-to tactic of the Philly Mob regarding anything outside of family issues. In the 1960s, the Philly Mob used violence and intimidation to great effect, allowing them to control various unions in the food and service industry and extort funds from a plethora of bars and restaurants. Still, Bruno's reign as Boss was predominantly one that "didn't rely on violence to get what [it] wanted," especially when considering the nature of the organization Bruno was leading and, because of this, "the Philadelphia rackets were never as profitable than when Angelo Bruno was in charge" (McKennett, 2019). This method of low violence and soft power was a far cry from the tactics of Bruno's predecessors and the violence that would subsequently come after Bruno's leadership ended.

The Gambino Connection

Bruno was rather reputable in the eyes of those in powerful positions within the Five Families of New York and the Commission. Indeed, he had used these connections to depose his predecessor and was the ideal choice of the Commission to take over as Boss of the Philly Mob. Perhaps this push by the Commission of Bruno came from his distinct juxtaposition with the chaos of those before him. Indeed, the Commission was now responsible for keeping at least a relative peace between the Mafia families, and they needed a Boss that could simmer the frequent boiling pot that was the Philly Mob up until this point. His connection to the Commission aside, Bruno also had one specific connection that proved integral to his retaining power and respect: Carlo Gambino. At the time of Bruno's appointment as Boss, Gambino was not only the Boss of the Gambino crime family but also the head of the Commission. To solidify the point of Gambino's influence, after his son's marriage to Tommy Lucchese's (another powerful mobster and Boss of the Lucchese crime family) daughter in 1962, both Gambino and Lucchese controlled the Commission and most organized crime operating in New York City. That kind of power and influence was integral for someone like Bruno, who was attempting to change the very nature of the organization he was leading. It also helped that Gambino shared Bruno's distaste for the trafficking of narcotics, regardless of the profits it brought in. With that in mind, Gambino would become Bruno's closest ally in the underworld.

Using his powerful connections, a knack for business, and close association with Gambino, Bruno developed and maintained respect from the other Mafia Bosses in the United States. With this, he cemented his position as the Boss of the Philly Mob. Speaking of connections, Bruno also rubbed shoulders with the glitzy and the glamorous, being "quick to indulge in the more glamorous parts of his lifestyle" (McKennett, 2019). In an interview, Jean Bruno (the daughter of Angelo Bruno) described her father's meeting with American superstar Frank Sinatra. When asked whether he had greeted Sinatra, Jean commented that Bruno replied as such: "No. He came up and said hello to me" (McKennett, 2019). Jean Bruno also revealed that she once saw her mother trying on expensive jewels that transpired to have once belonged to actress Marilyn Monroe. When questioned, she explained that Joe DiMaggio (star baseball player and ex-husband of Monroe's) had "been heartsick over [Monroe] and given the jewels to his close friend Angelo Bruno" (McKinnett, 2019). However, despite Bruno's Hollywood friends, powerful allies, relative immunity to law enforcement, and thriving criminal enterprises, the boiling pot he was charged with presiding over threatened to spill over.

Pressure Begins to Build

Though the power and respect commanded by Bruno served him well over his 21-year reign, pressure began to build around the armor of his reputation, and cracks began to form. As mentioned previously, Bruno preferred the more 'traditional' criminal activities conducted by the Mafia and disliked the rampant trafficking of narcotics, going as far as to ban Philly Mob members from participating in such activities. This drew the ire of many of Bruno's subordinates, who could not understand why Bruno held such an archaic viewpoint, especially when a large sum of money could be made. In fact, some Philly Mob family members went as far as to set up and run narcotic trafficking operations under Bruno's nose, one member being Harry Riccobene, who would later play a part in the ensuing power struggle after Bruno's exit. This ire from the Philly Mob members were exacerbated drastically as it became common knowledge that Bruno was allowing the Gambino family to sell heroin on Philly Mob turf in exchange for a cut of the profits, with Philly Mob members angered by the fact that they were not benefitting from the profits of the drug sales happening in their territory, but other criminal families were. These "strict limitations on the drug trade in Philadelphia" enforced by Bruno seemed, at least to the rank-and-file of the Philly Mob, to not apply to those who could line Bruno's pockets (McKennett, 2019).

It was not just the members of his own organization that began pushing against Bruno at this time. The newly burgeoning Philly Mob turf of Atlantic City, which was becoming increasingly profitable for Bruno's organization, was beginning to draw the attention of the major crime families. Bruno faced immense pressure from the Five Families of New York to allow them a cut of the rapidly lucrative market in Atlantic City. A market that expanded even further when, in 1976, gambling was legalized within Atlantic City, not only immensely increasing the flow of money into the Philly Mob's coffers but also "[making] the region more attractive to outside influences" (Hunt, 2023). However, the Five Families had a problem accessing the gambling enterprise. Due to long-standing Mafia rules, they could only enter into and operate within Philly Mob turf, in this case, Atlantic City, with the permission of the Philly Mob. Of course, this proved to be too much of a push for Bruno, who was unwilling to give such permissions.

As we can see, Bruno was facing pressure from all sides when the 1970s rattled forward into its later years, externally from the powerful Five Families of New York and internally from his rank-and-file members. Perhaps the final nail in the coffin of Bruno's reign came on October 15th, 1976, when Carlo Gambino died of a heart attack at his home in Massapequa, New York. While Gambino's death was not particularly unexpected, he was 74 years of age and had been suffering from heart disease. With his passing went Bruno's key ally in the underworld, triggering the bubbling pot under Bruno to spill over.

Bruno's Murder

Antonio Caponigro had been watching Bruno's ailing popularity closely. A 'made man' of the Philly Mob since the 1950s, Caponigro was the son of a wealthy banana merchant, hence his nickname 'Tony Bananas.' He had risen up the ranks of the organization and, by the 1970s, was Bruno's *consigliere*. From this position, Caponigro saw the end of Bruno's tenure as Boss looming and decided to not only hurry it along but to give the Commission a perfect replacement: Caponigro himself. Caponigro knew that he could rely on the support of numerous Philly Mob members after Bruno's death in his move for the rank of Boss and began to rally those within the Philly Mob who wanted a cut of the narcotics trade that Bruno vehemently denied them. With this in place and sensing the pressure beginning to bring Bruno down, Caponigro met with the Boss of the Genovese crime family and member of the Commission, Frank Tieri. The murder of key figures within the United States Mafia, while not out of the question when considering the protection of Mafia interests, was not to be taken lightly, especially in Bruno's case as a sitting member of the Commission.

In order to do so, Caponigro needed the authorization of the Commission, hence his meeting with Tieri. However, Tieri had his own motives in the deposition of Bruno. Caponigro had various profitable enterprises operating in Newark, New Jersey, where Tieri also ran his own operations. In an earlier challenge placed before the Commission to decide who retained control over the area, the Commission had sided with Caponigro in the territorial dispute, effectively ousting Tieri from operating in the area. So, when Caponigro approached Tieri regarding his scheme to kill Bruno and take control of the Philly Mob, Tieri began scheming of his own. Lying to Caponigro, Tieri told him that he would be able to vouch for him in the Commission and that his plan could go ahead with authorization. Caponigro put his plan into action, believing that his plan had been blessed and that his ascension to Boss was all but confirmed.

On March 21st, 1980, 69-year-old Bruno was sitting in his car not far from his house in South Philadelphia at an intersection, being driven by John Stanfa. Suddenly, a shotgun blast rang out, hitting Bruno on the back of the head. Bruno died instantly, while Stanfa was injured but ultimately survived. While "it is still unknown who exactly pulled the trigger," it is safe to say that the gunman was working on the orders of Caponigro (McKennett, 2019). The particularly brutal point is that Bruno's body sat in that car long after he had died and in complete view of the public. Reportedly, "people lined up in the street to get a glimpse of the infamous mobster, still sitting upright in the passenger seat" (McKennett, 2019). Surprisingly, images of Bruno's corpse at the scene of his murder are readily available on the internet. Be warned; however, they are not for the faint of heart. With Bruno's death came rampant chaos within the Philly Mob, but before we get there, Caponigro's story has one final act.

As soon as the Commission learned of Bruno's death, Tieri's scheme came to fruition. Called immediately before the Commission, Caponigro assumed he would be named as the new Boss of the Philly Mob. Imagine his surprise when, at the meeting, the Commission stated that the assassination of Bruno had not even been considered, let alone authorized. Surprised by this revelation, Caponigro turned to Tieri, desperately looking for support; for Tieri to tell them that it was, in fact, he that had given the authorization. Tieri denied ever giving such a blessing, and the Commission ruled that Caponigro had murdered a Commission member without authorization or, in other words, handed Caponigro a death sentence. Just under a month later, Caponigro's body, along with the body of his co-conspirator and brother-in-law Alfred Salerno, was found beaten and naked in the trunk of a car parked in the Bronx. Two other co-conspirators, John Simone and Frank Sindone were also murdered for daring to go against the Commission. For all that knew him, "Angelo Bruno will always be considered 'The Gentle Don,'" but the relative peace and stability of the Philly Mob under Bruno was shattered in all but a month. With the death of their Boss and *consigliere*, the Philly Mob devolved into chaos, creating a battleground where the next war for power would be fought.

CHAPTER 4
A STRUGGLE FOR POWER: THE SECOND PHILADELPHIA MAFIA WAR

The destruction and turmoil caused by the death of Angelo Bruno in 1980 and the effect this had on the hierarchy and structure of the Philly Mob cannot be overstated. The conflict known as the Second Philadelphia Mafia War lasted from Bruno's death until the mid-1980s, a four-year conflict filled with blood, subterfuge, and aggression. From the information laid out up to this point, it would be reasonable to assume that the violence apparent in the Philly Mob had subsided, the chaos giving way to order as the organization settled into place amongst the crime families of the United States. This assumption, however, is far from the truth. The death of Bruno acted as a gateway that opened up the Philly Mob to all manner of mayhem and disorder and saw the rise of one of the most violent and infamous mob Bosses to ever rule over organized crime in the United States. In this chapter, we will explore the state of affairs left in the wake of Bruno's demise, the details of the Second Philadelphia Mafia War, the tenure of two new Bosses: one short-lived and the other just beginning, and the structure of the Philly Mob as it comes to the end of the conflict in 1984.

Power Vacuum

With the loss of its Boss, *consigliere*, and some top *capos* (captains in the Mafia), the Philly Mob had a large space at the top of its hierarchy waiting to be filled. Quick to fill the gap themselves, the Commission accepted Bruno's underboss Philip Testa as the new Boss. Born in Philadelphia to Sicilian immigrants in 1924, Testa had been very close to Angelo Bruno, the two having met after living in the same area of South Philadelphia. Early law enforcement files on Testa describe him as a 'common gambler' in that his income was dependent on his winnings when gambling. Following the interesting pattern of mobsters being named after their birth family businesses, Testa was also known as 'The Chicken Man,' a nickname "that sprang from the Testa family poultry market" (Hunt, 2023). The nickname also may have been in regard to his distinct appearance, with Testa being described, somewhat candidly, as "[having] a face that only a mother could love" (Long, 2020) due to a supposed bout of chicken pox at an early age leaving his face scarred. The striking appearance of Testa aside, the new Boss of the Philly Mob began his reign in 1980, appointing Peter Casella as his underboss and Nicodemo Scarfo as his *consigliere*.

Testa's reign would only last a single year, ending in such a brutal way as to rival the death of his predecessor. In 1981, Testa was killed when a remote-controlled nail bomb exploded under the porch of his house as he attempted to open the front door. This killing was immortalized in the Bruce Springsteen song *Atlantic City*, the opening line of which is, "Well, they blew up the Chicken Man in Philly last night" (Springsteen, 1982). The 'they' that Springsteen is referring to are Testa's underboss Casella and *capo* Frank Narducci, who orchestrated the murder in yet another attempt to seize control of the Philly Mob. Earlier in the year, Testa, Narducci, and others were indicted on federal racketeering charges. Law enforcement speculated that "Narducci and Peter Casella arranged the bombing to take control of the Philadelphia Crime Family" (Hunt, 2023). This was not how the aftermath of Testa's killing panned out. Nicodemo Scarfo, himself eyeing the position of Boss, had his suspicions on who was responsible for the bombing, going directly to his friend and *consigliere* of the Genovese crime family Louis Manna and naming Casella and Narducci as the conspirators. In a meeting called by the Genovese family with Casella and Scarfo, Casella caved, ratting out Narducci and admitting his own involvement in the plot to take control of the Philly Mob. Casella, while escaping death, was subsequently banished from the Mafia, and fled to Florida. Narducci was not as lucky. In a revenge killing, Narducci was gunned down less than a year later by Salvatore Testa, son of murdered Boss Philip Testa, who was also a member of the Philly Mob and carved out a reputation for himself as a hitman, targeting those that had conspired to kill his father.

With all other opposers either dead or exiled, Scarfo had made himself the only viable candidate for the seat as Boss of the Philly Mob. He quickly gained the endorsement of the Commission, and by mid-1981, "his bloodthirsty reign had begun" (Patmore, 2022).

Nicodemo Scarfo Takes Power

Nicodemo was born in 1929 to Philip and Catherine Scarfo, Italian immigrants who had settled in Brooklyn, New York. When Scarfo was 12 years old, he and his family moved to Philadelphia, where the future mobster would spend his formative years. Nicknamed 'Little Nicky' due to his small stature, Scarfo began an amateur boxing career, participating in fights all over Philadelphia and garnering a reputation for his aggressive temper in the ring. After failing to make it as a professional boxer, Scarfo was "formally inducted into [the Philly Mob] in 1954" during the reign of Joseph Ida (Patmore, 2022). His uncle Nicky Buck, a Philly Mob soldier, had acted as his mentor, with Scarfo "being schooled in the Mafia life and trained to kill by one of the family's feared hitmen" (Patmore, 2022). As one might have already guessed, Scarfo's aggressive temper and difficult behavior were not exclusive to the boxing ring. In one instance, he refused to marry the daughter of Giuseppe 'Joe the Boss' Rugnetta, who was Angelo Bruno's *consigliere* until 1977, which left Rugnetta embarrassed and disrespected, causing a brief rift in the family. Then, one fateful day in 1963, Scarfo entered the Oregon Diner in South Philadelphia. Whether this trip was for business or leisure is lost to history, but Scarfo did neither, "taking exception to someone sitting in his preferred booth" (Patmore, 2022). The person in question was a 24-year-old longshoreman who engaged Scarfo, presumably defending his right to be seated in the booth. What exactly was said during this heated debate is another unknown factor; what happened next, however, is not. Scarfo grabbed a butter knife and stabbed the longshoreman to death. In the same year, he pleaded guilty to manslaughter for the fatal attack, serving ten months behind bars. Scarfo also served time in the early 1970s with his Boss Angelo Bruno and Louis Manna, whom he later called upon to dispose of his rivals after Testa's death. Even from Scarfo's history before his tenure as Boss, it is clear why Scarfo's rule over the Philly Mob was seen as "marked by violence and betrayal," and it was only just beginning (Patmore, 2022).

After Scarfo's ten-month sentence was up, Boss Angelo Bruno sent him to Atlantic City, New Jersey. There is much to be said about Scarfo in the context of Atlantic City, details of which are included in the next chapter. Suffice it to say that, in this new area, Scarfo carved out a very successful living for himself, creating the platform from which he set in motion his ascension as Boss of the Philly Mob.

Scarfo's Reshuffle

It is 1981, and Nicodemo 'Little Nicky' Scarfo has decimated all opposition and become Boss of the Philly Mob. Scarfo immediately appointed long-time friend and ally Salvatore Merlino as his underboss and Frank Monte as his *consigliere*. This was the beginning of a vast reshuffle in the hierarchy of the Philly Mob, with Scarfo appointing those he saw as loyal to him, or at least individuals he could easily control, and ousting those from powerful positions they had acquired under Scarfo's predecessors. Scarfo then proceeded to demote *capos* leftover from the reigns of Bruno and Testa, replacing them with his own, who included Phil Leonetti, Lawrence 'Yogi' Merlino, and Joseph 'Chickie' Ciancaglini. This reorganizing of the Philly Mob's hierarchy angered many members who, having enjoyed favorable positions under the leadership of Bruno and Testa, were less than pleased when they were, at best, looked over and, at worst, ousted when Scarfo took over.

Additionally, in order to further solidify his position, Scarfo allowed the families of the Commission to operate within Atlantic City (a chance they had been hungering for since the days of Angelo Bruno) in return for the Commission's continued support of Scarfo's legitimacy as Boss. Again, this drove the divide in the Philly Mob deeper, with members aggravated by Scarfo's allowance of New York gangsters to operate in Atlantic City. Scarfo spent almost two years of the Second Philadelphia Mafia War in prison on a gun possession charge. Not one to let a prison cell get in the way, Scarfo managed to run the Philly Mob in the same brutal fashion from his confinement. While locked up from 1982 to 1984 in the low-security Federal Correctional Institution, La Tuna in Texas, Scarfo was constantly flanked by two bodyguards. Referred to by Scarfo as his *'pistoleros'* (the Spanish word for gunfighters), these associates of the Mexican Mafia showed just how connected, powerful, and indeed dangerous Scarfo was, even when behind bars.

It is prevalent to note here that, while Scarfo was indeed Boss of the Philly Mob, this fact by no means meant that the landscape of the organization had begun to settle in any discernible way, with the Second Philadelphia Mafia War spilling over into the beginning of Scarfo's reign, not truly ending until 1984. In fact, it is arguable that the nature in which Scarfo had achieved leadership of the family, one of aggression, subterfuge, and violence, continued and even exacerbated the hostilities. Despite this divide in his organization, Scarfo managed to maintain control, albeit predominantly achieved through brutal crackdowns and bloody murders. There was, however, one final hurdle between Scarfo and his wish for a loyal and obedient Philly Mob, and that hurdle was about to make itself well and truly known.

No Tribute

During Scarfo's prison sentence from 1982 to 1984, a Philly Mob faction would begin to rise against him. Harry Riccobene, who had started his criminal career as a soldier under Salvatore Sabella in 1927, was a veteran of the Philadelphia underworld. Seeing the relative peace and stability of Angelo Bruno's reign fall into chaos and disarray after his and Testa's murders and disliking Scarfo's greedy nature, Riccobene was most definitely opposed to Scarfo as Boss of the Philly Mob. The straw that broke the camel's back, so to speak, came when Scarfo demanded tribute from Riccobene, a cut of the profits in his loan-sharking and illegal gambling enterprises. While customary, this greatly angered Riccobene as Angelo Bruno had allegedly never asked for a consistent or unreasonable amount of his profits, and that was precisely what Scarfo was expecting. Riccobene, as one can most likely tell, was not particularly keen on Scarfo, "[making] no secret of his disrespect for the new Boss" (Hunt, 2023). Thinking Scarfo to be an unfit and illegitimate successor to the position of Boss, Riccobene consequently refused to pay tribute. This sparked the Riccobene War, a sub-conflict of the larger Second Philadelphia Mafia war, a conflict that would cost Riccobene not only dearly but also finally cement Scarfo as the undisputed leader of the Philly Mob.

Riccobene was quick to strike where he knew it would hurt. His faction wrestled Scarfo for family control of all operations in Atlantic City. Knowing the extreme importance of the area in context to the family's profits, and with Scarfo currently in a Texas prison, *consigliere* Frank Monte hastily retaliated, telling his crew that they were to strip Riccobene of all his operations and take them for themselves. Monte did not stop there, approaching Mario Riccobene, Harry's half-brother, and ordering Mario to turn on Harry by leading him into a trap. This scheme of Monte's backfired, with Mario telling Riccobene about the murder plot. This move by Monte sealed his fate, as Riccobene, enraged by Monte's scheme, decided to strike first. Riccobene and Mario, along with hitmen Joseph Pedulla and Victor DeLuca, sat in a parked van across from Monte's parked Cadillac, waiting to spot him. After some hours, Monte appeared and attempted to enter his car. Pedulla fired three shots, killing Monte. The gang of hitmen, perhaps fueled by the momentum of their first hit, later attempted to murder Salvatore Testa, who, since the death of his father, had become a respected *capo* and deadly hitman working under Scarfo. This second assassination attempt would be unsuccessful, with the group being arrested by law enforcement.

Then came the death throes of Riccobene's insurgency against Scarfo's family. With all four men in police custody, someone was bound to squeal. That person was Mario Riccobene, who agreed to become a federal witness, testifying against Riccobene at the trial. He did this seemingly out of fear for his family, as his son had committed suicide out of fear of being killed by Scarfo in retaliation for his father's part in the murder of Frank Monte. Riccobene attempted to defend himself, stating that he had no involvement in organized crime, that the rumors of death threats made against them by Scarfo were just that, and that he was the one who actually tried to convince Mario, DeLuca, and Pedulla away from violence. All of his pleas fell on deaf ears, however, and Riccobene was convicted of first-degree murder and handed a life sentence. With Riccobene's imprisonment came not only the end of the Riccobene War but also the end of the larger war that encompassed it: the Second Philadelphia Mafia War. Through the brutal use of violence, aggression, and subterfuge, Scarfo finally crushed all those that dared to oppose his legitimacy as the Boss of the Philly Mob. The mob Boss still had six years of leadership left to live, and he was only just getting started.

CHAPTER 5
THE GAMBLER'S FALLACY: ATLANTIC CITY

Imagine, if you will, a series of coin tosses. You flip once. Heads. You flip again. Heads. A third time. Heads. A fourth time. Heads. What will the next toss be? Heads or tails? Many will say that it is more likely to be tails as the coin has landed on heads four times previously. However, this would be incorrect. The probability of any single coin toss is half and half. It does not matter how many times it has landed on heads previously; the chance is always the same: 50%. The assumption that the previous result of a coin toss is causally linked to the probability of the subsequent toss is an example of the gambler's fallacy. This example is relevant here as a way of representing the nature of Atlantic City in the context of the Philly Mob. Having been a part of the organization's sphere of influence as early as the territorial expansions of Joseph 'Joe Bruno' Dovi in 1936, Atlantic City was somewhat of a confusion for the Philly Mob, going from modest township to desolate backwater to lucrative metropolis as fast as one tosses a coin. The area was the backdrop for various enterprises, rackets, and infamous mobsters, and every criminal family in the United States wanted a piece. In this chapter, we will explore the history of Atlantic City, its relation to the criminal activities of the Philly Mob, and the way in which Nicodemo Scarfo used it to develop his stranglehold on the Philly Mob and rise to the rank of Boss.

Crime and Atlantic City

Nestled between islands and marshlands on the edge of New Jersey, looking out over the ocean, Atlantic City first adopted that name in 1853, when the idea came to develop it into a resort town. Due to its location, the area was noted as prime real estate as early as the 18th century, when the first hotel was built there. A building boom in the city came in the early 20th century, with hotels and businesses springing up across the landscape and down the famous boardwalk. Known for its casinos and beaches, Atlantic City is the inspiration for the United States version of *Monopoly*, the home of the Miss America pageant, and has attracted development from heavyweights such as Donald Trump. Criminal activity seeped into Atlantic City early in the 20th century, during the Prohibition era, which was enacted in 1919 and lasted until 1933. Considered by many to be Atlantic City's 'golden age,' alcohol flowed, and gambling took place in back rooms and basements of nightclubs and hotels, and the area came to be known as 'The World's Playground.' In subsequent decades, Atlantic City's fortunes entered a period of constant shifting, both economically and socially. Though still a popular tourist destination in the modern day, the area never saw a boom quite like that of the 1920s and, more prevalent to this exploration, its resurgence as a profitable enterprise in the late 1970s. Of course, wherever an economic boom is happening, the chance for lucrative business is also present. This attracted the burgeoning criminal organizations that were settling into the United States at the time, including the Philly Mob.

In the Prohibition-era environment, racketeer and political boss Enoch 'Lucky' Johnson rose to power, taking full advantage of the non-existent enforcement of Prohibition laws in Atlantic City, purportedly making annual kickbacks of $500,000 from illegal alcohol, gambling, and prostitution operations within the city. While not affiliated with the Philly Mob, Johnson was known to not involve himself in competing with other criminal organizations in matters of business or turf, preferring to take a cut of every operation running through the city instead. Johnson's real-life nature is a far cry from the fictionalized version of him seen in HBO's *Boardwalk Empire*, who murders his rivals and competes with mob Bosses for control of Atlantic City. The real Johnson simply facilitated other criminal organizations by running the political machine of Atlantic County that allowed the many crime families to operate within Atlantic City. That being said, his tendency to take a back seat in the running of criminal operations did not mean that Johnson was shy about being seen with known organized crime members. In May of 1929, Johnson hosted a conference for top organized crime figures in the United States. This meeting was the brainchild of Charles 'Lucky' Luciano, soon-to-be family Boss and orchestrator of the creation of the Commission two years later, and saw a slew of infamous gangsters descend upon Atlantic City. One particular guest of Johnson's was Al Capone, and the pair were snapped on a stroll together along Atlantic City's famous boardwalk.

Of course, the area of Atlantic City, despite being located a state over, had long been thought of as the turf of the Philly Mob. Dovi had expanded his family's operations into the area during the 1930s, and due to the city being in the Philadelphia Metro Area, the Philly Mob managed to retain control there. This stranglehold became tighter under Angelo Bruno, who fought off the advances of the Five Families of New York, who were attempting to cash in on the growing popularity of Atlantic City as a place for gambling activities and alcohol consumption. In fact, the pull of Atlantic City played a part in Bruno's murder, with mob Boss Frank Tieri falsely 'authorizing' Bruno's *consigliere* Antonio Caponigro to assassinate the Boss in order to eventually take over Caponigro's gambling enterprises and set himself up in Atlantic City. The Riccobene War, as part of the larger Second Philadelphia Mafia War, saw a rebellious faction of the Philly Mob attempt to wrestle control of operations in Atlantic City away from Nicodemo Scarfo, who, being incarcerated at the time, pushed back through his *consigliere* Frank Monte. Speaking of Scarfo, Atlantic City was also the backdrop in which he amassed his power and influence before making his play for the leadership of the Philly Mob, the details of which are covered later in this chapter. It is clear that, throughout the history of the Philly Mob up until this point, Atlantic City was both a lucrative beacon and a brutal battleground, ever shifting from one to the other.

Fall, Then Rise

After the initial boom of the 1920s fizzled out, along with the Prohibition laws, Atlantic City entered the era of nightclubs. Many popular nightclubs kept the area in the public zeitgeist through to around the 1960s when Atlantic City really began to suffer. Plagued by poverty, crime, corruption, and economic decline, Atlantic City became a ghost of its former self. The reasons for this downfall are many. It would not be completely inaccurate to place the blame at the door of both technological and social advances. At this time, World War II was still fresh in living memory, and a cultural shift was taking place in the United States. The automobile had become more readily available, and air travel dropped in price, expanding people's horizons and giving the individual more autonomy to choose where to travel and for how long. Culturally, the fast-growing popularity of suburbia played its part in Atlantic City's decline. With more and more families settling into private homes in suburban areas, they had luxuries such as swimming pools and air conditioning units at home, largely diminishing their need to travel to resort towns during the hot summers. As one can imagine, this drastically affected the landscape of the city, not only economically but also physically. Many of the great hotels that paved the streets of Atlantic City, and lined the famous boardwalk, were struggling with high vacancy rates towards the end of the 1960s. These once sprawling hotels were fated with either being converted into apartments or demolished entirely. In 1964, the Democratic National Convention was held in the city, the convention that nominated Lyndon B. Johnson for president. While this move was seemingly an attempt to save the ailing city (governor of New Jersey Richard J. Hughes had a close friendship with the Democratic presidential candidate), it only served the decline of the area further, with press coverage of the event highlighting to the general public the dire state of Atlantic City: filled with crime, poverty, and desolate buildings.

The overall decline of Atlantic City spelled disaster for the Philly Mob, who had been consistently operating in the area since the 1930s. By the 1960s, the area was viewed as somewhat of a backwater, a desolate place for any member of the Philly Mob unlucky enough to be sent there. While there were operations that continued to run in and through Atlantic City, they were small fry compared to the enterprises of the family back in the city of Philadelphia. That is until Atlantic City experienced a second wind, and that second wind blew strong. In 1976, New Jersey voters passed a referendum that allowed for the first legal casino outside of Nevada to be opened in Atlantic City. This was done in an attempt to revitalize a city on its last legs, which worked to great effect. Gambling had never been particularly popular in the context of the law in the United States. Predominantly, gambling had been explicitly outlawed in all of its forms, with those who had a proclivity for the pastime being forced to partake in secret. This was until legal gambling was introduced in the state of Nevada in the 1930s, setting the foundations for Las Vegas, which has survived to this day. When legal gambling came to Atlantic City, so did everything else, and rapidly so. Construction on new casinos started immediately, with them springing into existence up and down the boardwalk. Promoters, taking inspiration from Las Vegas, began bringing big-name boxing matches to the city to attract visitors to the casinos. Boxer Mike Tyson had the majority of his 1980s fights in Atlantic City, helping to push Atlantic City nationwide as a gambling resort. In six short years since the introduction of legal gambling, Atlantic City went from an unwanted backwater to a gambling metropolis. As we already know, Atlantic City was Philly Mob territory, and this resurgence had dollar signs all over it. The problem was that they were not the only criminal organization that knew it. Organized crime had become synonymous with casinos since their introduction in Las Vegas, and its connection to gambling had come even earlier. Atlantic City represented a lucrative business opportunity, and the keys were firmly in the hands of the Philly Mob. Amidst this fall and the rise of Atlantic City was a key individual we have already mentioned, and he would use this area well and truly to his advantage.

Scarfo's Stomping Ground

When Scarfo was released from prison in 1964, he "returned to the streets of South Philadelphia to unwelcome news" (Patmore, 2022). Bruno was extremely displeased with Scarfo. Brutally stabbing a longshoreman to death for no discernible reason was not a good look for the Philly Mob, especially under the leadership of 'The Gentle Don.' Bruno hated unnecessary violence, and Scarfo personified it, hence the friction between the two. As punishment, and perhaps to remove the unpredictable Scarfo from the main operations of the family, Bruno sent him to oversee the operations in Atlantic City. This was putting it nicely, as Atlantic City in the mid-1960s was not exactly a place where a burgeoning Mafia member could thrive. Scarfo had been banished for all intents and purposes and "may as well have landed on the Moon" (Patmore, 2022). Scarfo "scraped out a living with a bookmaking operation," living in the Italian area of Ducktown, Atlantic City. He was not alone, however, with his sister and mother living in the same apartment complex, along with Scarfo's young nephew and his future underboss Philip Leonetti. And this is where Scarfo stayed, away from the limelight of Philadelphia, where he could not cause the Philly Mob any more trouble. That was, however, until 1976.

When the introduction of legalized gambling hit Atlantic City, Scarfo made sure he would be catching the wave. Leonetti, who was in his early 20s at the time, recalled himself and his uncle Scarfo watching the announcement on television. During the announcement, New Jersey state governor Brendan Byrne had a provocative message for organized crime, exclaiming, "keep your filthy hands off our Atlantic City; keep the hell out of our state" (Patmore, 2022). As Leonetti puts it, after hearing Byrne's comment, Scarfo turned to Leonetti and said, "What's this guy talking about? Doesn't he know we're already here?" (Patmore, 2022). With this, the rise of Atlantic City as a gambling mecca would also see the rise of Nicodemo Scarfo as a powerhouse member of the Philly Mob, cementing his leadership of the organization. Together with his nephew Leonetti, Scarfo set up a concrete company called 'Scarf Inc.,' of which Leonetti was president, and a company called 'Nat-Nat Inc.' which installed steel rods that reinforced concrete. "No new casino would be built without either" (Patmore, 2022). Considering the multitude of new casinos being built to take advantage of the new gambling legislation, these companies proved very lucrative for Scarfo. This fact was doubly true as Scarfo would employ harsh intimidation tactics to force companies to buy their materials from him. This was typical of Scarfo, who, while known for idolizing fellow mobster Al

Capone, differed from him greatly in his style. Capone was known for his wit and charisma, while "Scarfo had neither," having "no sense of charisma; not even a hint of the old Mafia mystique" (Roberts, 2017). It is clear from the way Scarfo ran his enterprises, and indeed the way he ran the Philly Mob generally, that "Scarfo was a bully with a gun" (Roberts, 2017). Despite this rather unflattering character description, Scarfo's style worked wonders. *The New York Times* reported that, by 1987, Scarfo had made "$3.5 million through at least eight casino construction projects and other city infrastructure projects" (Patmore, 2022).

The construction business was not the only enterprise that Scarfo had a hand in. He employed more common mafia tactics in order to truly solidify his position as the dominant power in Atlantic City. He extorted money from the casinos he had helped build, controlling the local branch of the Bartenders and Hotel Workers Union through intimidation. With this, he could make sure that money kept flowing in the casinos by "[threatening] massively expensive labor disruptions" (Patmore, 2022). Perhaps unsurprisingly, intimidation also exploded into violence when, in 1978, Scarfo and Nicholas 'Nick the Blade' Virgilio murdered Judge Edwin Helfant "execution-style in a restaurant as he dined with his wife" (Roberts, 2017). Helfant was murdered after refusing to accept a $12,000 bribe to get Virgilio, who was facing murder charges at the time, a lighter sentence. While Virgilio carried out the murder, Scarfo acted as the getaway driver. Helfant's murder was a public execution, a message that showed what would happen if Nicodemo Scarfo did not get what he wanted. However, violence was not exclusive to not accepting bribes, as a contractor and frequent criminal associate of Scarfo's Vincent Falcone was killed on Scarfo's orders by Leonetti. His crime: making negative remarks about both Scarfo and his company. As Scarfo carved out an empire for himself in Atlantic City, the brutal conflict that would become the Second Philadelphia Mafia War was brewing. As we know, Scarfo was one side of that conflict, emerging victorious in 1984. With nobody standing in his way, his role as Boss of the Philly Mob secured by the Commission, and a host of lucrative enterprises in Atlantic City and beyond, Scarfo was one of the most powerful mob Bosses in the United States. But his unpredictability and hubris would catch up to him, and it would all come crashing down by the end of the decade.

CHAPTER 6
RUTHLESS AND PARANOID: NICODEMO 'LITTLE NICKY' SCARFO

By this point in the exploration, we have already been introduced to Nicodemo 'Little Nicky' Scarfo, his predisposition for violence, his casino empire in Atlantic City, and his victory against insurgencies within the Philly Mob when he took leadership of the organization. If we can believe anything so far, it is that Scarfo used brutal violence and shrewd business tactics to obtain his stranglehold of power and influence. However, it is infinitely harder to believe that this brutality not only continued but became much worse. George Anastasia, author and former journalist for *The Philadelphia Inquirer*, wrote this regarding Scarfo: "a greedy, ruthless despot whose family coat of arms could have been a pair of crossed .357 magnums mounted on a blood-red shield embossed with the words 'Kill or be Killed'" (Roberts, 2017). In this chapter, we will explore the Philly Mob during Scarfo's reign after he emerged victorious in 1984, his mental state during this time, and his eventual downfall, which saw even those closest to Scarfo turn against him out of fear.

The Mob Under Scarfo

Scarfo wasted no time shaping the Philly Mob to be an organization fit for him to rule over, using the criminal family as a weapon to beat anyone who dared cross him mercilessly. His goal was to unify all organized crime in his territory, creating a well-oiled criminal empire to rule over. Soon after becoming Boss, in a move that proved his "management style to be grounded in greed," he imposed a 'street tax' on all criminal rackets in Philadelphia and South Jersey, "even [from] petty criminals" (Roberts, 2017). This weekly tax came as a shock to many as, while extorting cuts from other criminals was a regular Mafia racket, it was considered unusual in Philadelphia, and those working independently from the Mafia were expected to pay. This gave Scarfo a hand in all manner of criminal activities, from drug dealing and pimping to bookmaking and loansharking. The price for not paying was the ultimate one, and Scarfo made sure that his soldiers dealt it out publicly and harshly. John Calabrese, loan shark, drug dealer, and pawn shop owner, was murdered by *capo* Joseph Ciancaglini and three other Philly Mob enforcers for refusing to pay Scarfo's tax. As was Frankie 'Flowers' D'Alfonso, who was brutally beaten by Salvatore Testa and Joey Pungitore before being murdered in 1985. Scarfo also ramped up the Philly Mob's influence on the labor unions in Philadelphia, just as he had done in Atlantic City. Having had a hold over the unions since the days of Angelo Bruno, Scarfo gripped them even harder. The Philly Mob maintained degrees of influence over the local branches of numerous unions: the Roofers Union, the Iron Workers Union, the Labor Union, and the Teamsters Union, using this stranglehold to siphon funds from unions and extort businesses. This was an extremely efficient racket for the Philly Mob, as it was very little work in return for massive payouts and benefits.

Scarfo was also extremely eager to involve the family in the methamphetamine trade. While the family dabbled in the trafficking of cocaine and marijuana during this time, meth was a drug that had become very popular in the Philly Mob's territory. Popularity equaled money, so it was integral to Scarfo that his organization take control of the illicit trade. This takeover started simply enough, with the Philly Mob beginning to extort money from local meth dealers. The Philly Mob then began supplying phenylacetone, colloquially known as P2P and the key ingredient to the manufacturing of meth, furthering their control of the drug trade. This did present a benefit to some criminals who began borrowing money from Scarfo's organization to finance their meth operations and hence started to work with the Philly Mob instead of being extorted by it. With control of the supply of P2P, the Philly Mob could generally keep on top of the meth trade in their territory. However, it was when Chelsais Bouras, Greek-American gangster and Boss of the Philadelphia Greek Mob, attempted to cut in under Scarfo on the methamphetamine trade in Philadelphia that matters became more complicated. On top of this, he also refused to pay Scarfo's 'street tax' for operating on Philly Mob turf. Enraged by this blatant disregard for his power and reputation, the hot-headed Scarfo ordered Bouras to be publicly killed for all to see. He wanted Bouras's murder to be an example to all other local criminal organizations that the Philly Mob was top of the pile. He decided this despite the fact that the Philly Mob had a lucrative history of working closely with the Philadelphia Greek Mob and that a proportion of his own family members were, in fact, involved in Bouras's drug trafficking operation. Whether Scarfo was aware of this fact or not is of little consequence. The only thing that mattered to him was making it abundantly clear to all of the primacy of the Philly Mob in all criminal enterprises that operated in his territory. So, as Bouras was eating dinner with company, including his girlfriend and even one of Scarfo's own soldiers Raymond Martorano, a gunman appeared at the table and shot Bouras to death, killing Bouras's girlfriend in the process. One can imagine that the collateral damage of the hit was of no consequence to Scarfo, who only cared about the message it sent: he was Boss, and people would do well to respect it.

The Mind of a Mafia Boss

There is a story about Nicodemo Scarfo that perfectly encapsulates his psyche, one of pure ruthlessness and aggression. Reportedly, "he [Scarfo] was once said to have exclaimed 'I love this. I love it' with joyous excitement while watching his soldiers tie up the body of an associate he's ordered killed for insulting him by underestimating his power" (Patmore, 2022). There is nothing better than this that describes the mob boss so wholly yet with brevity. Indeed, this unpredictable and volatile nature ultimately led to Scarfo being ousted from the seat at the top of the Philly Mob. However, before we get there, it is important that we catch a glimpse of the inner workings of Scarfo's mind. Nicholas 'The Crow' Caramandi, a member of the Philly Mob under Scarfo, became a government witness towards the end of Scarfo's reign after being caught by the

Federal Bureau of Investigation (FBI). In a *Time Magazine* interview, he described, amongst many things, what it was like to know Scarfo. Caramandi explained that "if you were in good graces with him, he loves you and you love him. But you never knew from one day to the next. He'd turn on anybody, and he drew no lines when it came to killing" (Behar & Caramandi, 1991). It seems that even those closest to Scarfo were never fully sure as to his motives and next actions, with "even an unwitting sneer [provoking] him to take violent revenge" (Roberts, 2017).

Indeed, Caramandi's statement regarding Scarfo's psyche can be reinforced by his actions during the mid-to-late 1980s. During this time, Scarfo "ordered the murders of nearly 30 members of his own family" (Patmore, 2022). One of these members was Pasquale 'Pat the Cat' Spirito, who was only inducted into the Philly Mob for two years until Scarfo ordered his killing. Little is known about Spirito's early life. The son of Stephen and Rose Spirito, he hailed from the Italian community of Chambersburg in New Jersey. Introduced to the criminal underworld by Joseph Ciancaglini, Spirito passed himself off as both a plumber and hardware store owner to mask his criminal activities. When involved in loan sharking and bookmaking operations during his early criminal career, he became a close associate of Harry Riccobene and his half-brother Mario, earning his nickname 'The Cat' due to his abilities as a con artist, possessing an attractive charm and demeanor. Remaining an associate of the Philly Mob, Spirito got his chance to become a full-fledged member when he acted as the getaway driver in the shooting of John Calabrese, after which he was inducted as a 'made man' into the organization under Philip Testa, along with Francis

Iannarella and Andrew DelGiorno. Despite his close connection to the Riccobene brothers, Spirito had switched sides during the Riccobene War, aligning himself with Scarfo. Due to this change of loyalty, Spirito was almost killed when he was fired upon while driving his Cadillac down the street, the gunman working for Harry Riccobene. This attempt on his life was also in retaliation for the brutal murder of Samuel 'Little Sammy' Tammburino, who was shot 16 times after leaving his parents' pharmacy in South Philadelphia by Charles Iannece and Francis Iannarella. After Scarfo took power, Spirito worked under him as a hitman and recruiter, taking on associates Caramandi, Charles Iannece, and Ralph Staino Jr. before presenting them to Scarfo as 'proposed members'. It is speculated that it was this fact that rubbed Scarfo up the wrong way regarding Spirito, with Philip Leonetti (Scarfo's nephew and late-reign underboss) later stating that Scarfo was furious at Spirito for suggesting who should be made *capos* and soldiers, feeling insulted that his underling was telling him how to run the organization. When Spirito later hesitated when Scarfo ordered him to kill Richard Riccobene, Harry Riccobene's brother, Scarfo snapped and ordered a hit on Spirito. Perhaps for a hint of irony or poetic justice, Scarfo chose Caramandi for the job, on which Caramandi said, "what was I gonna do? It was kill or be killed. There was no 'no'" (Behar & Caramandi, 1991). Caramandi went on to describe the brutal nature of killing those close to you, explaining, "Pat had bad vibes and knew what was coming. He had me in this booth in a luncheonette drinking coffee for four hours, making me tell him how much I loved him, and it's already set up to kill him the next night" (Behar & Caramandi, 1991).

Scarfo was beginning to become notorious for his ruthless nature and paranoid demeanor, constantly shifting his feelings about his closest associates, himself severely paranoid about dishonest and disloyal underlings. With any hint of perceived disrespect or insubordination came swift and brutal retribution from Scarfo, usually by close family members in a public setting. Caramandi states that "Scarfo was a cowboy. He didn't want a guy taken into a house and shot easily in the back of the head. He wanted it outside, in broad daylight, with a million people around. Restaurants, funeral homes, anywhere. Then it gets written up in the papers, and it puts fear in people. He loved that cowboy stuff" (Behar & Caramandi, 1991). With the number of murders associated with organized crime rising exponentially during his reign, it was clear that the Philly Mob under Scarfo was unsustainable. It would only be a matter of time before the organization Scarfo desperately held onto would turn against him. As Caramandi said, "he [Scarfo] was very, very paranoid. He betrayed himself" (Behar & Caramandi, 1991).

Scarfo's Downfall

The fact that Scarfo was ordering the murders of his own loyal family members did not go unnoticed. However, it was the 1984 killing of Salvatore Testa that truly saw the grip Scarfo had on the Philly Mob begin to loosen. The son of former Boss Philip Testa, Salvatore Testa had proven himself "an extraordinarily efficient and loyal captain" under Scarfo (Patmore, 2022). Scarfo had allowed Testa to avenge his father's murder, with Testa personally seeing to the killing of many of the conspirators in his father's murder.

However, the paranoid and obsessive Scarfo began to worry about the young hitman, believing him to be "rising too fast" and becoming popular enough within the Philly Mob that Scarfo thought he would eventually make a move against him. Salvatore Merlino, Scarfo's underboss, had a daughter that was engaged to be married to Testa. In 1984, the year of his murder, Testa broke off the engagement, angering Merlino. Caramandi, who eventually helped in the killing of Testa, stated this regarding the event: "Salvie [Testa] figured that by marrying the daughter of the underboss, he'd be right at the top. But she was a spoiled brat, and a couple of months before the wedding, he backed out. When Salvie backed out, he signed his own death warrant. It was a blow to the underboss. This was the ultimate insult. That night, it's time to leave, and [Merlino] grabs Salvie by the neck and kisses him on the lips. That was the kiss of death" (Behar & Caramandi, 1991). Using this as his reason, Scarfo jumped at the opportunity to get rid of Testa, permitting Merlino to murder him. On September 14th, 1984, Testa's body was found by law enforcement "bound by rope and wrapped in a blanket" at the side of a road in New Jersey (Patmore, 2022). While it is reasonable to assume that Scarfo was more than happy with the death of Salvatore Testa, it solidified his reputation to other members of the Philly Mob, and indeed all other criminal organizations in the United States, as a disloyal, paranoid, untrustworthy, and dangerous individual. Caramandi, while being directly involved in the killing, encapsulates the wider feeling of Philly Mob members on the death of Testa when he stated, "It was just awful. We killed him in a candy store. I really liked him. There was no reason for it" (Behar & Caramandi, 1991).

Even with his reputation rapidly decaying, Scarfo continued to crack down on his own organization. After underboss Merlino's drinking problem became too much of a liability, Scarfo demoted him to the rank of soldier and appointed Philip Leonetti to the position. However, even Leonetti was beginning to turn against his uncle, "being disgusted" at Scarfo's actions regarding Testa (Patmore, 2022). In 1985, Scarfo sent Caramandi, along with a few other associates, to extort $1 million from real estate developer Willard Rouse. Rouse immediately contacted the FBI, who began an operation to take down Scarfo once and for all. During this undercover operation, the FBI sent in agents under the guise of being Rouse's representatives. This operation ended with Caramandi, who was indicted for his part in the extortion, turning on Scarfo and testifying against the Philly Mob. This opened up the Philly Mob, making Scarfo vulnerable to law enforcement, snowballing between 1987 and 1989 as charge after charge was brought against him; three charges stuck: racketeering, conspiracy, and first-degree murder. One by one, "Scarfo's men started defecting to the government," with Tommy DelGiorno joining Caramandi in testifying to receive both shorter sentences and avoid retribution from the ruthless Scarfo (Patmore, 2022). Finally, the final nail in the coffin was hammered in when Philip Leonetti, who was facing a 45-year prison sentence and "wasn't going down for his uncle," agreed to testify against him (Patmore, 2022). All in all, 15 Philly Mob members received prison sentences ranging from 30 to 55 years, including Scarfo himself.

Ruling Behind Bars

Scarfo received consecutive prison sentences of 14 years, 55 years, and life for his convictions. Although the life sentence was ultimately overturned (he was acquitted in a second trial for the murder charge), Scarfo became known as "the first Mafia Boss to be sentenced to death" (Roberts, 2017). Scarfo began his sentence in 1989 at the Atlanta State Penitentiary. During the trial, Scarfo's personal life also suffered. His youngest son, Mark Scarfo, at only 17 years of age, attempted suicide in 1988. Having been bullied relentlessly by peers and classmates about his father's criminal activities and becoming increasingly depressed by his father's possible imprisonment, Mark hanged himself in Scarfo's concrete company office in Atlantic City. While his mother did find him and paramedics were able to resuscitate him, Mark's brain had been deprived of oxygen for too long as he suffered a cardiac arrest. He fell into a coma, which he remained in until his death in 2014.

The convictions against the wider Philly Mob had devastating effects, with "Scarfo's actions [decimating] the Philadelphia family" (Patmore, 2022). As the 1980s came to an end, so did Scarfo's bloody reign, fueled by paranoia and violence. Law enforcement had managed to cut off the head of the Philly Mob, and much more, with 21 members incarcerated, 11 under indictment, and six turned government witnesses. In a report by the Pennsylvania Crime Commission, it was estimated that only 24 members of the Philly Mob were not facing charges and were freely operating. With so many of Scarfo's men serving long prison sentences and only a small amount of boots on the ground in regard to Philly Mob members, the Five Families, and the Commission acted quickly to avoid another power vacuum in the organization. John Stanfa was endorsed to take over the Philly Mob as Boss. From his cell in Atlanta, Georgia, Scarfo learned of his deposition as Boss and that Stanfa had replaced him. Although never truly shaking off his criminal ways (he was named in a companion indictment to the extortion of a Texas-based financial group as recently as 2011), Scarfo died of natural causes behind bars in 2017, never again to walk the streets he controlled, stained with blood and chaos.

CHAPTER 7
THE WAR TO END ALL WARS: JOHN STANFA AND THE THIRD PHILADELPHIA MAFIA WAR

Nicodemo Scarfo's nine-year reign had left the Philly Mob in ruin. With the majority of their members either in prison, awaiting sentencing, dead, or working with law enforcement, the prospects of the criminal family of Philadelphia were not looking bright. With considerable influence from the Genovese and Gambino crime families, the Commission was quick to appoint John Stanfa as the new Boss, hoping to avoid yet another war for control of Philadelphia. In somewhat of a self-fulfilling prophecy, a war is exactly what they got. Against the backdrop of a long war-torn territory, a new battle would take place for the coveted space at the top of the Philly Mob, and after the smoke had cleared, a new kind of Philly Mob would emerge. In this chapter, we will explore the appointment of John Stanfa, the rising of another insurgent faction within the Philly Mob, the details of the Third Philadelphia Mafia War, and the development of a new type of leadership entirely.

The Appointment of Stanfa

John Stanfa was born in Sicily in 1940 and was brought up surrounded by Mafia affairs. His brothers had all become *mafioso*, being 'made men' in the Gambino crime family. Emigrating to the United States at 23 years old, he listed his occupation as a bricklayer. After arriving, he settled with his wife in New York City, where he was quickly introduced to the Gambino crime family by his brothers and brother-in-law. It was arranged by the leaders of the Gambino family that Stanfa would work for Angelo Bruno, then Boss of the Philly Mob. So, by the late 1960s, Stanfa found himself in Philadelphia under Bruno. It is not entirely clear how often Stanfa was tasked with chauffeuring Bruno around, but this definitely was his job on March 21st, 1980. If it was just a task handed to him randomly that day, then Stanfa was quite the unfortunate man, as this was the day that Bruno was assassinated. Bruno took a shotgun blast to the back of the head while sitting in the passenger seat of his car just outside his home. While Bruno was killed instantly, Stanfa was injured in the shooting. There is no hard evidence to suggest that Stanfa had a hand in the slaying of Bruno, but there is at least some circumstantial evidence. He had rolled the window of the car down, supposedly so Bruno could smoke. However, an open window would have also given the gunman a clear shot at Bruno.

Perhaps Stanfa was not unfortunate after all and was placed there as part of the killing. Regardless, if Stanfa was involved in the conspiracy to kill Bruno, it was his connection to the Gambino family that most likely saved him from retaliation, as conspirator Antonio Caponigro was himself murdered by the Commission for the same crime. Stanfa was then called to testify before a grand jury concerning Bruno's killing, disappearing shortly afterward, again with the help of his connections. In December of 1981, however, he was found in Baltimore, Maryland, working as a baker in a pizza shop. Unceremoniously dragged back to Philadelphia to face charges, Stanfa was accused of lying to the grand jury regarding his role in the slaying of Bruno after it was revealed that Stanfa had meetings with mobsters soon after the death. Charged with perjury (falsely affirming an oath to tell the truth), Stanfa was sentenced to eight years in prison, serving six of those years. Free to walk the streets of Philadelphia again in 1987, Stanfa was soon appointed as the new Boss of the Philly Mob after the chaotic reign of Nicodemo Scarfo ended in a large portion of serving family members ending up in prison in 1989/1990. However, history tends to repeat itself when those do not learn from it, and there were certain Philly Mob members that did not take kindly to Stanfa's appointment.

A Divide in the Family

The repeated intrusion of the New York families into the business of the Philly Mob caused friction within its ranks. Many of the younger mobsters in the organization were Philadelphia-born and took displeasure in the appointment of Stanfa. While being of Italian descent was still a prerequisite for membership in the Philly Mob, the Mafia tradition of Italian-born leadership had waned as the organization had modernized. Hailing from Italy and settling in New York under the protection of the New York families, Stanfa was seen as not having worked his way up the Philly Mob hierarchy and not understanding the territory in the same way as the

Philadelphia-born members did. One Philly Mob member had this exact opinion. Joseph 'Skinny Joey' Merlino was the son of disgraced former underboss Salvatore Merlino, born in Philadelphia in 1962. His birth family was rife with connections to the wider Philly Mob: son to Scarfo's underboss and brother to Maria Merlino, who was briefly engaged to Salvatore Testa before the hitman's breaking off of said engagement and eventual murder. He was also close friends with 'made men' the Ciancaglini brothers Michael and Joseph, whom he had met during his school years.

It could be said that Merlino was raised specifically for a life in the Philly Mob. He first butted heads with the law in 1982, when Merlino and Salvatore Scafidi beat and stabbed two restaurant patrons in Atlantic City, with Merlino being found guilty of aggravated assault and possession of a weapon for an unlawful purpose. Two years later, Merlino was banned by the New Jersey Casino Control Commission from entering any New Jersey casinos, the same sentence being leveled at his father later that year. Salvatore Merlino would then, in 1988, be sentenced to 45 years in prison as part of the broader indictment of Scarfo-era Philly Mob members. A year later, in 1989, Joseph Merlino would follow in his father's footsteps, but with an altogether different outcome.

In October of 1989, Nicky Jr., son of imprisoned Boss Nicodemo Scarfo and member of the Lucchese crime family, was shot in Bella Vista, Philadelphia. Hit eight times, but not in any vital organs, Nicky Jr. survived, and no one was ever charged with the attempted murder. That being said, the FBI and local law enforcement had a theory that placed Merlino as the orchestrator of the shooting. There was some bad blood between the Scarfos and Merlinos, and police informants have pointed to Merlino as the triggerman in the shooting. Apparently, Merlino "deliberately dropped the gun that night because he wanted to send a message" to Nicodemo Scarfo, who was incarcerated at the time (Anastasia, 2013). Scarfo was, as one can imagine, a big fan of gangster movies, one of his favorites being *The Godfather*. In a move identical to a scene in the movie, the gun was left at the restaurant. Merlino allegedly did so to show the elder Scarfo that he no longer had any power in Philadelphia. "Merlino had a score to settle that night," or at least, that is the leading theory of law enforcement (Anastasia, 2013). Merlino himself denied involvement in the shooting, claiming to have been under house arrest on the same night for an unrelated charge. Since his curfew was 7 p.m. each night, Merlino stated that he could not have been the shooter, "hardly a solid alibi, but his position nonetheless" (Anastasia, 2013). Years later, a rumor on the streets purported that, from prison, Scarfo had put a $500,000 bounty on Merlino's head in retribution for the attempted slaying. When asked by TV reporter Dave Schratwieser about the bounty, "Joey calmly looked into the camera in that classic Merlino-style and said, 'Give me that half million dollars and I'll shoot myself'" (Anastasia, 2013). Surprisingly enough, it was not this event that landed Merlino in prison. His incarceration was instead due to his involvement in an earlier crime where $352,000 was stolen from a Federal Armored Express Truck. This crime occurred in 1987, and in January of 1990, Merlino was convicted of planning the heist of the truck and subsequently sentenced to three years behind bars.

It was during this prison term that Merlino met Ralph Natale. A fellow Philadelphia-born mobster, Natale shared Merlino's feelings on John Stanfa. Both men felt that, due to Stanfa's connections to New York organized crime and the fact he had been in prison for the majority of Scarfo's reign in the 1980s, he was unfit to lead the Philly Mob. This is where the two insurgents hatched their plan to seize control of the organization from under Stanfa. There were other key conspirators in the plot: Michael Ciancaglini, Stephen Mazzone, George Borgesi, Gaetano Scafidi, and Martin Angelina. The rebellious Merlino faction would later be dubbed by the press as 'The Young Turks.' Stanfa, however, was aware of this divide in his organization. To appease Merlino's faction, Stanfa appointed Michael's older brother Joseph Ciancaglini as his underboss, hoping that this would bring Merlino and his supporters under the wider banner of Stanfa's Philly Mob and, by doing so, avoid yet another bloody internal conflict. However, this did very little to ease tensions. In 1992, another brutal civil war was fully in the swing for control of the family, known as the Third Philadelphia Mafia War.

The factions traded blows quickly and violently. Stanfa's loyal *capo* Felix Bocchino was murdered first, followed by a swift retaliation by Stanfa, who ordered the killing of Michael Ciancaglini, Merlino's right-hand man. The attempt on Ciancaglina's life failed, with Michael narrowly avoiding a hail of gunfire outside his home by diving inside and taking cover. The other Ciancaglini brother was not as fortunate. Having been appointed as Stanfa's underboss, young Joseph Ciancaglini found himself on the opposite side of the war to his brother. In 1983, Joseph was shot by three Merlino faction gunmen while managing his restaurant in South Philadelphia. While he did not die, he was left in a vegetative state by the brutal attack, the Merlino faction delivering a devastating blow to Stanfa with Joseph's incapacitation. Stanfa did not wait to strike back, sending gunmen to kill Merlino himself. In August of 1983, as Michael Ciancaglini and Merlino exited a social club, a car pulled up next to them, and the occupants opened fire. Merlino was shot four times and walked away, injured but alive. Michael was not lucky enough to cheat death a second time, being shot directly in the chest and dying. Not even a month later, a drive-by shooting was performed on Stanfa and his son. Driving on the Schuylkill Expressway, a van pulled up beside Stanfa's car and unleashed a hail of bullets. Stanfa escaped uninjured, but his son was shot in the jaw, only surviving as Stanfa's driver managed to lose the assailants and get them to a hospital. Stanfa's faction continued to attempt on Merlino's life, with Stanfa gunman Philip Colletti later testifying that he had planted numerous remote bombs under Merlino's car, none of which evidently had successfully gone off. In November of 1993, Merlino was sent back to prison, charged with violating his supervised release.

Bugged and Jailed

Merlino's 1993 incarceration seemed like a win for Stanfa's faction. With the leader of 'The Young Turks' imprisoned, perhaps he could finally wrest control of the Philly Mob back and rule over a stable organization. Like many best-laid plans, however, this was not what happened next. While Merlino was supported by young mobsters he had known from childhood, Stanfa struggled to find the manpower from within the Philly Mob, as many were serving long prison sentences or killed after the Scarfo era. In an unusual move, Stanfa began recruiting criminals and hitmen who were not of

Italian heritage, which broke a longstanding Mafia tradition, to maintain control of the organization and its territory and fight the ongoing war against Merlino's faction. With this being his main priority, "Stanfa brought in people who had no background in the mob but who were willing to break legs and pull a trigger" (Raab, 1995). Two of these individuals were the Veasey brothers: John and William. John Veasey would be the one who was intrinsic in dismantling Stanfa and his control over the Philly Mob. In 1994, Stanfa and 23 of his associates were indicted on multiple charges, from loan sharking and labor racketeering to murder. This came within seven years of the indictment of Scarfo and his associates, becoming the second federal indictment of the Philly Mob in so many years. Stanfa's indictment specifically holds the title of the largest prosecution of an organized crime group in Philadelphia history.

This prosecution was not something Stanfa could just shake off. The authorities had a key piece of evidence that deeply implemented Stanfa in all charges brought against him and his men. This evidence was two years of recordings taken of Stanfa as he explicitly discussed mafia business with mobsters in both his attorney's and doctor's office. Believing that attorney-client privilege and doctor-patient confidentiality would protect him from anything he said leaking, Stanfa would openly discuss business in these places, warts and all. What Stanfa did not know was that the FBI had obtained a warrant to bug both places after deducing that the offices were being used as meeting places for Philly Mob business.

Consequently, they had heard everything and had proof. With this overwhelming evidence stacked against them, Stanfa's men began to squeal. The Veasey brothers agreed to testify against Stanfa. On the day of Stanfa's trial in 1995, William Veasey, who was scheduled to testify against Stanfa, was murdered. A similar fate nearly befell his brother, but John Veasey escaped and gave the authorities information that secured Stanfa and 20 of his men's convictions. In July of 1996, Stanfa was sentenced to life imprisonment, which he still serves today at 82 years of age. With Stanfa imprisoned, along with many of his associates, it was time for Merlino, having been released from prison in 1994, to take his place as the leader of the Philly Mob. Merlino, however, decided to do things differently than those before him. Merlino named Ralph Natale, who was also out of prison, as the new Boss, positioning himself as Natale's underboss. While on the surface, it seems like a strange move to make, Merlino had a plan. Natale would serve as a distraction, someone for law enforcement to fixate on, while he pulled the strings from behind the scenes, away from prying eyes.

'Front Boss' Natale

A fellow Philadelphia-born mobster, Ralph Natale's father was an associate of the Philly Mob, running a numbers operation for the family. Natale himself was mentored by notable Philly Mob hitman Felix 'Skinny Razor' DeTullio, who "operated out of the Friendly Lounge where Natale tended the bar as a young man" (Burnstein, 2021). Under DeTullio's tutelage, Natale carved out a "formidable reputation as a racketeer and enforcer" for Angelo Bruno during the 1960s and 1970s, being Bruno's point man within the labor unions, specifically the Bartender's Union Local 170 (Burnstein, 2021). Former union leader Joseph McGreal demanded that Natale be removed from his leadership position, presumably suspicious of Natale's ties to the Philly Mob. McGreal was found dead in 1973, murdered, and Natale continued to help Bruno maintain control in the labor unions by "traveling around the country troubleshooting and greasing palms" (Burnstein, 2021). According to Natale, he became a 'made man' of the Philly Mob at a secret ceremony in Manhattan, attended by Bruno and Carlo Gambino, continuing to support Bruno as he expanded the organization's operations in Atlantic City through "a hostile takeover of bartenders, construction, and hotel and casino workers unions" (Burnstein, 2021). Natale also did not shy away from getting his hands dirty if requested, murdering conman George Feeney in 1970 on the orders of Bruno after Feeney began talking disrespectfully about Natale and Bruno.

Natale went to prison in 1979, just as Bruno started losing his grip on the Philly Mob. Convicted of arson and sentenced to 12 years, Natale was also convicted a year later for his part in the drug deal of 500,000 quaaludes and 10 kilograms of cocaine, for which his sentence was upgraded to 15 years. While in prison, he collided with Merlino, and the two began plotting their insurgency against Stanfa's Philly Mob. Although not released until 1994, Natale was still active during the Third Philadelphia Mafia War, "[commanding] a war that left a trail of bodies" (Burnstein, 2021). In 1990, he ordered a hit on two individuals: bookmaker Louis 'Louie Irish' DeLuca and James 'Jimmy Brooms' DiAddorio, who were murdered within four months of each other. Released on parole in 1994, Natale found himself "as the don of the Bruno-Scarfo crime family" (Burnstein, 2021). He can be linked to two more murders in his tenure as Boss. One was in 1996 when Natale had North Jersey *capo* Joseph Sandano murdered for refusing to attend two separate meetings. The final one being Anthony Turra, who, before being able to come to trial for conspiring to kill Merlino, was found shot to death outside of his house. Natale's time as Boss of the Philly Mob was not what it seemed to be, with his underboss Merlino having far more power than his rank would have suggested. However, as much as he thought it, Merlino was not safe, as we will see that the influence of the law can be as far-reaching as that of crime.

CHAPTER 8
THE POLITICS OF CRIME: RALPH NATALE AND JOSEPH MERLINO

From the Natale-Merlino era onward, we not only begin to see a shift in the way the Philly Mob as a criminal organization is run but also some key individuals whose presence is well and truly alive in the organization today. Natale's title of Boss was indeed only a title, the real power behind the Philly Mob being held by Merlino. This setup could have been the winning one for Merlino. However, his predisposition for flamboyance and love of media attention allowed the long arm of law enforcement to infiltrate the Philly Mob right at its highest levels. In this chapter, we will explore the events of the Natale-Merlino era, Merlino's personality as the "John Gotti of Passyunk Avenue," and the reasons for Natale's eventual betrayal of his own organization (Anastasia, 2013).

The Puppet Boss

"Moving into a luxury condo along the Delaware River in New Jersey," one would imagine that, in the fall of 1994, Natale felt on top of the world (Burnstein, 2021). Having commanded and won a war for control of the Philly Mob, been given the title of Boss of the organization, and been released from prison, Natale set up his headquarters at the Garden State Park Raceway, "holding daily meetings at the restaurant on the building's top floor" (Burnstein, 2021). Unbeknownst to Natale, the FBI had the condo and restaurant bugged for "virtually his entire reign" (Burnstein, 2021). How much Natale knew of Merlino's power over him is unclear. Perhaps it did not matter, with Natale being perfectly content with his position. Or perhaps Natale saw it differently, thinking that the title of Boss would supersede all else and that he would always hold more power and influence than Merlino. Intriguing speculation aside, Natale did not just rest on his laurels during his four-year reign as Boss. While Merlino predominantly ran the organization, Natale positioned himself favorably within political circles. He managed to gain leverage with Milton Milan, mayor of Camden, New Jersey, "funneling the young politician with $50,000 in bribes" (Burnstein, 2021). He also began dabbling in the illicit drug trade and entered into an extra-marital affair with "one of Merlino's female contemporaries who was friends with his daughter" (Burnstein, 2021).

On the other hand, Merlino was not wasting any time in using his power. Merlino "[handled] collections and shakedowns in Philly," as well as overseeing the more general activities of the Philly Mob, that being gambling, loan sharking, extortion, and stolen goods rackets. He also spent this time developing beneficial relationships with other criminal organizations, such as the Pagans MC (of whom Merlino was good friends with the president Steve 'Gorilla' Mondevergene) and the Junior Black Mafia, of which Merlino was close with numerous members. The Pagans MC also acted as muscle for Merlino when underworld disputes broke out, further proving Merlino's intrinsic influence on the group. During the 1990s, Merlino would also avoid death numerous times, as hit after hit was attempted on him. In 1995, the leader of the Philadelphia drug gang, the tenth and Oregon Crew Louis Turra, was severely beaten and had his Rolex watch stolen by men working for Merlino for failing to pay the street tax on the drug money earned by the gang in Philly Mob territory. Merlino was doubly invested in teaching Turra's crew a lesson in respect, as they had also been warring with the Pagan MC motorcycle club. Turra was angered by the beating he received and wanted retribution. Turra's father, Anthony, organized a meeting at his house where he, Louis, and members of the 10th and Oregon Crew plotted to murder Merlino. This plot failed to come of anything, however, as father and son were both indicted in 1997 on many charges, including the conspiracy to kill Merlino. While awaiting trial in a New York prison, Louis Turra was found dead in his cell, allegedly having committed suicide by hanging himself in 1998.

It is heavily speculated that the Philly Mob (or indeed the wider Mafia) had a hand in Louis Turro's killing. What is more apparent is the death of the elder Turro that same year. In March, Anthony Turro (61 years of age and battling terminal cancer that bound him to a wheelchair) was mercilessly gunned down outside of his home by a gunman in a black ski mask. Anthony Turro was leaving his house that day to attend the federal courthouse, where a jury was deliberating on the charges against him and four others. In a statement from law enforcement, it was clear that they believed the shooting of Anthony Turro was a mob assassination. We know from the last chapter that Natale was linked to the elder Turro's murder, reportedly ordering the hit himself. Perhaps the Philly Mob was sending a grave message. Crossing them, or even thinking about crossing them, would be punishable by death.

Merlino's Notoriety

While 'Front Boss' Natale provided a face to the Philly Mob as a distraction for law enforcement, Merlino's plan required him to work behind the scenes, holding power in the shadows by not drawing too much attention to himself. For anyone that knows even the smallest amount about Joseph Merlino, it will come as no surprise to find out that this is exactly the opposite of what Merlino did. Merlino gained a reputation as a flamboyant celebrity gangster, not unlike John Gotti or Al Capone, comparisons with which Merlino would most likely be very pleased. He was often seen at the fanciest locations, partying with a large entourage. The comparison to Gotti came from his candid and carefree demeanor in front of the camera. Indeed, unlike other mobsters, Merlino loved the media's attention. He would invite the press to philanthropic events he hosted, like "Christman parties for the homeless and [giving] away turkeys at Thanksgiving in the housing projects" (Anastasia, 2013). Being a "celebrity wise guy," Merlino was known for his general demeanor when interviewed, with his "dark eyes that can shoot daggers and the quick, staccato delivery when he's telling a story or asking a question" (Anastasia, 2013). Merlino loved the celebrity life, flaunting his power and influence whenever and wherever he got the chance. Still, like many of the fast-talking and wise-cracking mobsters throughout history, Merlino had a dark side. He never explicitly said it, but it was behind his eyes at all times, implicit in every conversation he had. He was powerful. He was dangerous. And he wanted people to know it.

Merlino was notorious for flashing cash and making huge bets with bookies. The problem was that Merlino refused to pay when he lost. This practice is known as guzzling, and Merlino single-handedly managed to pull this stunt at both mob-controlled and independent bookies. Merlino's continued flamboyant and reckless behavior began to grate on the wider criminal underworld. Through the arrogance and aggression of Merlino and his Philly Mob, many criminal gangs and individuals were unwilling to work for or cooperate with them. In June of 1998, after a short stint as Boss, "FBI agents arrested Natale at his condo on a parole violation" (Burnstein, 2021). Perhaps expecting his long-time friend and collaborator to give him aid, Natale did not panic. That is, until Merlino almost immediately took control of the Philly Mob, stopping all support for the imprisoned 'Boss,' "cutting him out of the loop" (Burnstein, 2021). This betrayal was devastating for Natale, who was now left facing charges with no support or contacts, having been "put on the shelf" by his own organization (Burnstein, 2021). However, if this betrayal was devastating, Natale's counter would serve to split the Philly Mob wide open, and Merlino was in his crosshairs.

King Rat

Having been left high and dry by his former insurgent and ally, Natale was extremely incensed. As an instant reaction, he offered to secretly record conversations with Merlino. This, however, never materialized, and it was not until September of 1999 that Natale was able to gain any leverage in regard to his predicament. After being hit that year with an indictment in prison for "pushing crystal meth" (Natale had a hand in the sale of illicit drugs since his ascension as Boss), Natale "felt no particular loyalty to Merlino and spilled the beans on their entire operation" (Burnstein, 2021) in order to gain a more favorable sentence. With this decision, Natale became the first sitting Boss to become a government witness in American Mafia history. From 1999 to 2001, Merlino, his underboss Stephen Mazzone, his *consigliere* George Borgesi, Martin Angelina, John Ciancaglini, and a slew of other Merlino men were arrested and put on trial for various crimes: racketeering, illegal gambling, loan sharking, extortion, murder, and attempted murder. Reading like a comprehensive list of mafia organization activities, the proceeding trial was highly publicized. Originally, Merlino was only indicted for drug offenses (one count of conspiring to distribute more than five kilograms of cocaine and one count of unlawful use of a communications facility in relation to a drug trafficking offense), but this was later expanded to include the racketeering, murder, and attempted murder charges, one of which was for orchestrating the murder of Anthony Turro in 1998.

Just as in other eras of the Philly Mob, in the face of overwhelming charges and the prison sentences that came with them, many of Merlino's former associates and allies agreed to work with law enforcement, testifying against Merlino in order to receive lighter punishments themselves. Of course, there was Ralph Natale, but also many others peeled off from Merlino into the waiting hands of the authorities. Gaetano Scafidi struck a deal with police in 2000 while in prison because of fears that he would be killed by Merlino upon release. After being charged with two murders, Peter Caprio agreed to cooperate in the same year. Ron Previte, who was already working as an undercover informant for law enforcement by the time of the trial, also gave evidence. All of the turncoats testified that both Natale and Merlino had conspired and plotted to start a mob war with John Stanfa's faction in order to take control of the Philly Mob and that Merlino himself had participated in numerous criminal acts throughout the 1990s. Natale, during his testimony at Merlino's 2001 racketeering trial, also gave evidence as to the involvement of Merlino in numerous murders during the 1990s. However, "Merlino might have gotten the last laugh" as "Merlino allegedly kept Natale in the dark regarding details of certain murders carried out on his watch" (Burnstein, 2021). This withholding of information goes to show the shrewdness of Merlino's plan to install Natale as Boss while keeping the power for himself. Natale could not use information against him if he did not know it in the first place. "The jurors didn't buy everything the animated former mob Boss was selling on the stand." Consequently, Merlino was acquitted of all murder charges (Burnstein, 2021).

Merlino did not get off freely, however. When the jury returned a mixed verdict after hearing all testimony, Merlino was acquitted of all counts of murder: three counts of murder and two counts of attempted murder. He was, however, immediately found guilty of racketeering charges, including bookmaking, extortion, and receiving stolen property. Six of Merlino's associates were found guilty of various racketeering charges also. In December of 2001, a judge handed Merlino a sentence of 14 years. In response, Merlino clapped back, "Ain't bad. Better than the death penalty" (Press,

2001). Merlino was almost caught with a murder charge a month later when he was indicted again for the murder of Joseph Sodano, even though a jury found the murder charge 'not proven.' Later, in 2004, however, Merlino was acquitted of Sodano's murder. Taking his cooperation with law enforcement into account, Natale was given 13 years for drug dealing, racketeering, and bribery. He had admitted to committing eight murders and four attempted murders, so one could argue he got off with a light sentence. He started his prison time in 2005, being released six years later in May of 2011, where he was entered into witness protection. In his later life, Natale released a book entitled *Last Don Standing: The Secret Life of Mob Boss Ralph Natale* in 2017. In January 2022, at the age of 86, Natale passed away from natural causes.

CHAPTER 9
TO FLEE A SINKING SHIP: RATS

In the Mafia, loyalty will get you far. We only need to refer back to the opening quote of this book from Joseph Bonanno, who himself was the Boss of a crime family, to see that loyalty and reliability are desirable traits. To become a 'made man' in any criminal organization, those in power must trust you unconditionally, and if they trust you, they will protect you. That is the way that you survive and thrive in organized crime. That is, until it is not. After seeing Ralph Natale, who has the rather unceremonious title of "the mafia Boss who flipped," it seems pragmatic to now explore some of the multitudes of members and associates of the Philly Mob that broke the trust of the Philly Mob, turning on their family members predominantly in order to save themselves from the law. The fact of the matter is that, regardless of loyalty, crime is fickle. An individual's fortunes change rapidly and without warning. Besides, in a dog-eat-dog world that is an organized crime family, neither loyalty nor selfishness is guaranteed to keep you alive, and one must roll with the punches. In this chapter, we will explore some of the more prevalent and intriguing turncoats that have attempted to turn the Philly Mob over to the authorities throughout its history. From a corrupt police officer and a child mobster to a bulletproof rat and a psychopath's personal hitman, these accounts highlight the brutal, unforgiving world of organized crime and the lengths one must go to try and survive.

From Cop to Bouncer to Soldier: Ron Previte

When Ron Previte returned to the United States after his time in the United States Air Force, he joined the Philadelphia Police Department. However, Previte was a bad cop. Depending on your definition of the word, this could mean many things. Suffice it to say that Previte became corrupt, saying that "he learned the most about how to be a criminal while working as a cop" (Anastasia, 2017). Born in 1943 in Philadelphia to Sicilian-American parents, Previte was raised in Hammonton, New Jersey. During his time in the Air Force, Previte served in Vietnam before returning to Philadelphia and joining law enforcement. During his time in the police force, Previte busied himself with activities that were arguably the opposite of what a cop should be doing, extorting traffic violators, shaking down restaurant owners, stripping impounded cars, stealing from crime scenes, and soliciting payoffs from bookies and mobsters (Roebuck, 2017). Moral implications aside, Previte was keeping himself busy. Unsurprisingly, he was forced to retire from the police force in 1979, saying, "I was asked to leave, but they never had enough to charge me with anything" (Anastasia, 2017). Two years later, Previte found himself working security at the Tropicana Casino & Resort in Atlantic City. Being "six-foot tall and sometimes 300 pounds, Previte was an imposing and intimidating figure," making him perfect for the job (Anastasia, 2017). One would also assume it helped immensely in Previte's criminal activities, which continued into his role at the casino. As an associate of the Philly Mob by this time, Previte stole chips and cash, stole all manner of items from the casino warehouse, robbed guests, and ran prostitutes and poker games out of unoccupied suites. As Previte puts it, he was "robbing the place blind" (Anastasia, 2017).

It was around this time that John Sheeran, a detective for the New Jersey State Police, began taking notice of Previte, who was fast becoming "a major and independent player in the underworld" (Anastasia, 2017). Sheeran started building a case against Previte, and after being arrested for theft in 1985, he agreed to begin working with law enforcement in exchange for the charges being dropped. Due to his work with the Philly Mob, the FBI also collared him to work as an informant, for which Previte was paid $750,000 from 1992 to 2002. The 1990s was when Previte got involved fully in the Philadelphia crime family when the mob had "replaced respect and loyalty with deceit and treachery, no longer a thing of honor," as Previte put it (Anastasia, 2017). By 1993, by using his abilities as a "shrewd and astute underworld entrepreneur," Previte had buried himself deep in the Philly Mob, earning big money, becoming a 'made man,' and even landing the role of Boss John Stanfa's personal driver. Previte fed information to the FBI and law enforcement throughout this time, wearing wires for the better part of two-and-a-half years. He later described his time wearing wires on a daily basis as "the most exciting time of his life" (Anastasia, 2017). With this information, law enforcement was able to indict and charge Stanfa and a large part of his crew. Though coincidental, this also saved the lives of many Natale-Merlino faction members, who were locked in the bloody internal conflict of the Third Philadelphia Mafia War at the time with Stanfa and his men.

After Stanfa's crew were indicted in 1994, Previte managed to align himself with the new regime of Natale and Merlino. While many of the faction's members, in hindsight, claim to "have been suspicious" of Previte, this would not be a problem for Previte, who alleviated any suspicions by bringing envelopes stuffed with cash to Natale and Merlino, provided to him by the FBI (Anastasia, 2017). Again, Previte fed information to authorities through the use of wires. These recordings (more than 400 hours' worth of conversations with Natale, Merlino, and others) were integral to the eventual downfall of the Natale-Merlino Philly Mob. "Faced with secretly recorded Previte conversations that placed him in the middle of FBI-monitored drug deals," Natale had little choice but to plead guilty and testify for the government (Anastasia, 2017). The recordings that included Merlino also helped to charge him with racketeering despite no murder charges sticking.

All in all, Previte's work as an informant for law enforcement helped to imprison over 50 mobsters, many of whom were members and associates of the Philly Mob. Refusing offers to join witness protection, Previte returned to live in Hammonton, explaining his rationale with "I like it here" (Anastasia, 2017). There he stayed until his death from a heart attack in 2017, aged 73. If there is anything to end the story of Ron Previte on, it is this: "Ron Previte always lived life on his own terms" (Anastasia, 2017).

Childhood Mobster: Phil 'Crazy Phil' Leonetti

Philip 'Crazy Phil' Leonetti should have had it great. While his father had abandoned him and his mother, she brought him up herself. The two of them moved to Ducktown, a predominantly Italian-American part of Atlantic City, from his birthplace in Philadelphia. And it was not just him and his mother; Leonetti had his uncle to watch over him in Ducktown, who was also a very prominent member of the Philly Mob. On paper, it seemed as though Leonetti would get a perfectly good start in life. But his uncle was Nicodemo Scarfo, who would go on to tear a hole in the Philly Mob's territory and fill it with blood, anger, and chaos on his way up to the top of the pile. Being connected by blood, Scarfo would bring his nephew Leonetti along for the ride. Appearing to be the direct opposite of his uncle Scarfo, Leonetti was calm, quiet, and reserved, both as a child and into adulthood. His nickname 'Crazy Phil' is somewhat of a red herring, given to him by a radio talk show host in 1973. Leonetti was not a fan of the name, and none of his Philly Mob associates referred to him as such.

Despite this picture of a reserved and laid-back person, Scarfo seemed to be adamant about inducting his nephew into the world of organized crime as early as he could. Leonetti alleged that when he was eight years old, Scarfo asked his mother whether he could take young Leonetti out for a drive. Of course, the young boy begged his mother to say yes. His uncle even said that he could sit up front with him. As they drove, "Scarfo told his nephew of the dead body in the trunk. He was a bad man, Scarfo explained, and sometimes you had to take care of men like this" (Patmore, 2022). Leonetti went on to explain that, after his uncle had brutally stabbed a man to death with an icepick in New Jersey for disrespecting him, he had used young Leonetti as a decoy as law enforcement were less likely to stop and search a car with a child in it. This fact was told to the young boy by Scarfo, and Leonetti said that it made him "[feel] special, like he was really helping his uncle" (Patmore, 2022). And, with that, "Leonetti had been sucked into his uncle's orbit. And for the next 25 years, he would rarely leave Scarfo's side" (Patmore, 2022).

Leonetti benefited from his uncle's position in the Philly Mob. Leonetti was president of 'Scarfo Inc.,' his uncle's concrete company. Also, by the early 1980s, and at around 30 years of age, Leonetti was a millionaire, controlling lucrative enterprises in loan sharking, racketeering, illegal gambling, extortion, and skimming money from the Atlantic City casinos. This reputation and wealth did come at a price, however. In 1979, Scarfo ordered Leonetti to kill Vincent Falcone, and he did so, shooting Falcone twice. This was far from the only murder Leonetti was involved in, later admitting to his part in 10 additional murders. A year later, Leonetti was officially inducted into the Philly Mob as a 'made man.'

As feelings of war began to bubble to the surface of the organization after the death of Philip Testa in 1981, his uncle Scarfo jumped at the chance to seize power, which he eventually did through aggressive and ruthless means. Later, in 1986, Leonetti would even be made Scarfo's underboss. However, Leonetti (along with many of Scarfo's other *capos* and high-ranking associates) had already begun to fear Scarfo's temper, paranoia, and unpredictability. After Scarfo's murder of his own loyal *capo* Salvatore Testa, Leonetti knew the situation was crumbling rapidly. "Testa's murder meant that nobody was safe, and Leonetti grew weary of his uncle's suffocating presence" (Patmore, 2022). Leonetti never got a break from Scarfo, as they lived in the same building, and Leonetti had become Scarfo's personal chauffeur, driving him everywhere he went. When Scarfo went to prison from 1982 to 1984, Leonetti described it as "the happiest period of [his] mob life" (Patmore, 2022). In 1988, when Leonetti was convicted of racketeering and 13 murders along with Scarfo and other Scarfo-era Philly Mob members, Leonetti decided that enough was enough. In what Scarfo saw as the ultimate betrayal, Leonetti (who was facing a 45-year sentence) "flipped and entered witness protection, becoming a very effective witness against Scarfo" (Patmore, 2022). This led to the conviction that put Nicodemo Scarfo away for the rest of his life. In a media interview in 1996, when asked how his uncle thinks of him, Leonettie replied, "I guess I never would be dead enough for him. If he could keep killing me, he would be a happy guy" (Patmore, 2022). For his part in the Scarfo-era Philly Mob's activities, Leonetti received 45 years. In 2013, after his release from prison, he released the book *Mafia Prince: Inside America's Most Violent Crime Family and the Bloody Fall of La Cosa Nostra*, which detailed his criminal life.

Headshot Survivor: John Veasey

John Veasey's father was a violent alcoholic. When he was found dead in a hotel room in 1970, Veasey's mother, Sophia Maria Cuticchia, was left to support five children alone, of which John was the youngest. Veasey's eldest brother, William, became somewhat of a surrogate father to him, despite only being five years his senior.

Unfortunately, Veasey's life did not get any easier from there, with Veasey saying, "we started fighting very young" (Cipriano, 2010). Fiercely protective of their mother, who was a bartender and continuously suffered from the unwanted advances of suitors, Veasey recalls when he was nine that, William, who was 14, "woke him up one night and handed him a stick, so the brothers could club into submission a boyfriend who had smacked their mother around" (Cipriano, 2010). The Veasey brothers were known to be tough street fighters, working out at the Goodfellas Gym at 16th and Passyunk in their hometown of Philadelphia. In the gym, John found that he had a knack for weightlifting, reportedly being able to power-lift 365 pounds. Despite his obvious physical talent, John was constantly bullied for the difficulties he faced as a student. "People told him he was stupid," and John seemingly believed them (Cipriano, 2010). Attempting to find other outlets, John fell into drugs, smoking marijuana at 11 and taking his first injection of meth at 14. It was around this time that John Veasey first fell onto the radar of law enforcement.

At 15, John was arrested after an incident at school. He had pulled a knife on one of his teachers and was charged with both aggravated assault and making terroristic threats. A year later, he was moved to St. Gabriel's Home for Boys after Cuticchia died of a heart attack at 41. Veasey's drug problem worsened, "turning to crime to support a cocaine habit that escalated to $600 a day" (Cipriano, 2010). William did attempt to support John at this time, albeit in the only way he knew how. William would beat up John if he caught him getting high and would also "beat up neighborhood drug dealers who sold to his kid brother" (Cipriano, 2010). In 1990, 24-year-old

John Veasey was arrested for beating his wife's ex-husband, a beating so vicious that it ultimately led to the man's death. For whatever reason, the death was ruled as a drug overdose, and Veasey pleaded guilty to related charges, serving two years before being paroled in 1993. When Veasey was released from prison back into his home city Philadelphia, he would soon find himself "smack in the middle of the bloodiest mob war in the city's history" (CBS News, 2013). Boss of the Philly Mob John Stanfa was warring with an upstart faction of young mobsters led by Joseph 'Skinny Joey' Merlino, and between law enforcement and the ongoing conflict, Stanfa was running low on muscle. John Veasey, who now worked as a laborer at a concrete company, was a "rock-hard 200-pound slab of muscle" by this point and was all the muscle that Stanfa needed (Cipriano, 2010).

It was Stanfa's underboss Frank Martines that first approached Veasey about working for the Philly Mob. Martines offered Veasey $10,000 to kill Merlino, and he readily accepted the job. Martines told Veasey that he could have some time to think it over, but Veasey retorted, "take some time to get me a gun. And let's get it done" (CBS News, 2013). And, with that, John Veasey became a hitman for the Philly Mob. Stanfa, who was struggling to keep the family in order during the war with Merlino, was on a recruitment frenzy and, with Veasey, got "a guy who wasn't afraid to go out there and bust heads, and a guy who would go out and kill people if he was ordered to do so" (CBS News, 2013). Veasey and Phil Coletti were driving around the city, Coletti up front and Veasey in the back, on the hunt for Merlino. They found him on a street corner, chatting away with his right-hand man Michael Ciancaglini and a few others. Taking a closer look, Veasey spotted his brother William in the group, who was a childhood friend of Merlino's. Veasey told Coletti that they could not strike yet as his "brother would see [him]" (Cipriano, 2010). The pair drove around the block until only Merlino and Ciancaglini were left. As they strolled down the street, Veasey and Coletti pulled up beside them in their Ford Taurus. Unleashing a hail of bullets, the hitmen managed to kill Ciancaglini and wound Merlino.

After successfully killing Merlino's right-hand man and wounding the insurgency leader himself, Stanfa continued using Veasey as his muscle. Veasey also murdered popular bartender Frank Baldino as Stanfa felt that he was "[becoming] too friendly with the other side and wanted him dead" (CBS News, 2013). Veasey, although admitting that he liked Baldino, "shot him six times in the head" to make sure he was dead" (CBS News, 2013). Veasey also collected money for Stanfa, claiming that "he never once had to use brutal force on a shakedown" as "people paid because of his reputation" (Cipriano, 2010). Veasey proved this reputation when he was told by his brother William that he had overheard mobster (and cousin of underboss Martines) 'Joe Fudge' talking openly about killing Veasey. Inviting Fudge to his house, where Veasey was under house arrest and had to pick up a call from his parole officer, Veasey used a paddle-tipped power drill to rip out chunks of Fudge's hair as well as a baseball bat to strike at his knees. This example of Fudge was all being made while Veasey sat on the phone with his parole officer, the pre-recorded message "asking Veasey to repeat the names of American states in a precise order to prove it was John Veasey live on the phone" (Cipriano, 2010). Veasey's star was rising under

Stanfa and the Philly Mob, but soon the tide would turn, and Veasey would find himself in the hands of law enforcement.

Still having not been paid his $10,000 for the hit on Merlino and Ciancaglini, Veasey began to question Stanfa as to why. The only money he was earning was a weekly payment of $300, which was less than his paycheck as a laborer. These complaints "did not sit well with Stanfa," however, and Stanfa then ordered a hit on Veasey himself (CBS News, 2013). When he learned that his little brother was in trouble, William, using his connection in the Philly Mob, warned Veasey and pleaded with him to work with the cops "to become a government informant: a rat" (CBS News, 2013). So, from 1994, at the behest of his brother, that is exactly what Veasey did. As part of his deal with law enforcement, Veasey agreed to wear a wire and collect evidence. He was not, however, wearing one on a fateful night in January of 1994, when Veasey was lured to an apartment in South Philadelphia by two men he trusted: Martines and *capo* Vincent 'Al Pajamas' Pagano. When he stepped into the apartment, everything was covered in plastic. "It's not normal to walk into a room with plastic," Veasey explained later, "but I did. I never thought anything" (CBS News, 2013). If he did not suspect anything, then he surely did when Martines and Pagano attacked him. Veasey was shot three times in the head and once in the chest by Martines. But John Veasey, as we have seen, was a fighter. Miraculously, Veasey survived the gunshots. When Martines then came at him with a knife, Veasey "wrestled the knife from [him], stabbed him, and ran from the building" (CBS News, 2013).

After surviving the assassination attempt, Veasey became a legend in the underworld. As George Anastasia explains it, "this is a guy who can't be killed now. And that enhances that whole reputation as a tough guy. John Veasey should have been dead that night, and he wasn't. I don't know [how it happened]. Maybe it's destiny. Maybe this was supposed to happen" (CBS News, 2013). Not that Veasey stayed in the Philadelphia criminal underworld after this. Entering the witness protection program in 1994, Veasey testified against Stanfa and his men, helping secure a conviction that put Stanfa away for life. His brother, William, was scheduled to do the same. He was, however, killed on the day of Stanfa's trial. Veasey was given ten years for his part in crimes committed during his work with the Philly Mob. Ever since his brother's murder, Veasey has been adamant that the Ciancaglini family is to blame. John Ciancaglini, along with others, was tried in 2001 for William's murder but was found not guilty. Veasey is now married to his wife of eight years, Norma, and became a car salesman, a job in which he seems to excel at, being nicknamed 'The Closer' due to his ability to "[sell three times as many cars as the average salesman" (Capriano, 2010). He lives under an alias after leaving the witness protection program, and "few in his new community are aware of his past" (CBS News, 2013). Far away from his old life as a Philly Mob hitman, Veasey claims that he has left organized crime behind him, stating, "like I say now, I'm not who I want to be. I'm not who I'm gonna be. But I'm definitely not the person that I used to be" (CBS News, 2013). However, many doubt Veasey's capacity for change, from crime reporters to residents of his old operating ground of South Philadelphia. Commenting on Veasey's new-found religious beliefs, George Anastasia ponders, "he's found God because it's expedient to find God, because he's somewhere in middle America, and it works to find God there. I don't think that if he's back on a street corner in South Philly, he's found God. He's looking to avenge what happened to his brother. He's looking to settle scores" (CBS News, 2013). Indeed, Veasey has made explicit threats against the Ciancaglini family, with John Ciancaglini's wife, Kathy, saying that Veasey has been intimidating her for years. "He believes that my husband has killed his brother," she states, "he threatens me, calls my husband a punk. He's the punk. He threatens women. It's what he does" (CBS News, 2013). It seems that only time will tell whether John Veasey has truly left his criminal past behind him or whether the pull of vengeance will prove too strong.

Scarfo's Hitman: Nicholas 'Nicky Crow' Caramandi

A hitman and soldier during the reign of Nicodemo Scarfo, Nicholas 'Nicky Crow' Caramandi witnessed the bloody regime of Scarfo destabilize and eventually break the Philly Mob. From his position as Scarfo's top hitman, Caramandi watched as Scarfo, fueled by greed and paranoia, began systematically murdering his crime family members. Fearing his own head was soon to be on the chopping block, Caramandi, along with others in the Scarfo-era Philly Mob, such as Tommy DelGiorno and Scarfo's nephew and underboss Philip Leonetti, turned themselves over to law enforcement. While we have previously covered the reign of Scarfo in other chapters, it is prevalent here to briefly cover Caramandi's role in the wider activities of the Philly Mob at this time as well as his role in the eventual imprisonment of the ruthless crime Boss. Much of this information comes from a *Time Magazine* interview with Caramandi by American journalist Richard Behar, where

Caramandi spoke at length about his time in the Philly Mob and his dealings with Nicodemo Scarfo.

Caramandi was recruited to the Philly Mob by Pasquale 'Pat the Cat' Spirito in the early 1980s, just as Scarfo took control of the organization. Spirito suggested that Caramandi, along with Charles Iannece and Ralph Staino Jr., become members of the Philly Mob, presenting them to Scarfo for approval. Unhappy with this (Scarfo was notoriously insecure and felt Spirito was questioning his authority), Scarfo ordered Spirito to be killed, and Caramandi was roped in to carry out the murder. As Caramandi explains, "We tried for months to kill him, and for a while, that's all we used to talk about. We used to get sick when we'd see him. We'd want to throw up" (Behar & Caramandi, 1991). Becoming suspicious, Spirito attempted to talk to Caramandi to put his mind at rest. Caramandi, rather coldly, reassured Spirito that everything was fine, leaving Spirito relieved. This conversation happened the day before Spirito's murder. "We killed him in a car. Shot twice in the back of the head", said Caramandi, remembering the hit, going on to say, "I went round the corner to a bar and waited till it came on the TV news at 11. I said, 'Christ, they killed my best friend.' I was pretending like I was crying. This was my alibi. 50 people would have sworn I was there [in the bar] since 8 p.m." (Behar & Caramandi, 1991).

Caramandi also participated in the infamous murder of Salvatore Testa. This murder was the key to a large portion of Scarfo's inner circle turning on him out of fear. When asked about the murder of his friend Testa in the interview, Caramandi's eyes began to tear up. He explained, "You love him; you gotta do it. 'This thing' comes first. It comes before your mother, your father, your sister. It's the name of the game. If you're a gangster, you gotta be a gangster. You never know who you're gonna be told to kill in this business" (Behar & Caramandi, 1991). Caramandi's reaction to the assassination of Testa was similar to many members of the Scarfo-era Philly Mob, who felt that Scarfo had gone too far as Testa was a loyal and effective *capo*, his only perceived crime being that he was becoming too popular for Scarfo's liking. Giving further details about his role in the murder, Caramandi states, "I helped drag his body out, threw him on a road in Jersey, and left him in a ditch with a blanket wrapped around him. I seen his face when I turned the car around" (Behar & Caramandi, 1991). Suffice it to say, the murder affected Caramandi deeply, "I used to get nightmares over Salvie and would wake up in cold sweats screaming his name. This went on twice a week for three months" (Behar & Caramandi, 1991).

It was not just Scarfo's orders that bothered Caramandi and his fellow family members, however, as it seemed clear to them that Scarfo's psyche was unraveling right before their eyes. Describing Scarfo, Caramandi said, "He held grudges. If you didn't say hello to him 20 years ago, he never forgot. He used to say 'I'm like a turtle. I get there'" (Behar & Caramandi, 1991). Scarfo's soldiers and associates were terrified of him, and Scarfo made sure he knew what his underlings were thinking at all times. As Caramandi explains, "What Scarfo would do was take everyone to dinner and order double margheritas. Then he'd start talking about people, wants to see who chimes in, wants to see what they got to say. He'd make a guy drink and drink and talk and talk until there was no more talk left in him. I never talked because I knew this was a trap" (Behar &

Caramandi, 1991). In 1985, Caramandi was sent by Scarfo to extort $1 million from real estate developer Willard Rouse. The FBI was informed immediately, and Caramandi was collared by law enforcement. As Caramandi puts it, "It wasn't my will to be a rat. I was arrested after the FBI had wired my construction partner for 18 months. I was in jail, and I believed I was gonna be killed there. I was scared to death. I was shaking. I blame Scarfo. He's the guy that wanted to kill me" (Behar & Caramandi, 1991).

In 1987, Caramandi pleaded guilty to murder, racketeering, and conspiring with a Philadelphia councilman to extort a real estate developer. In order to receive a more lenient sentence, and indeed to protect himself from Scarfo, Caramandi testified at 11 trials and helped with 52 convictions, including that of Nicodemo Scarfo, who was sentenced to life in prison. In regard to his feelings on his actions against the Philly Mob, Caramandi said, "all my life, I was a stand-up guy. I was loyal; I killed for the guy [Scarfo]; I brought him millions of dollars. There's no way I was ever gonna turn. It never even entered my mind. [But] you don't realize how precious a life is until you're in that position where you're gonna get killed, and you'll do anything to survive. I loved some of them guys. And I had to point the finger and bury them" (Behar & Caramandi, 1991). With this, Caramandi helped put away one of the most violent and ruthless mob bosses to ever operate in the United States Mafia, throwing the powerful Philly Mob into chaos.

CHAPTER 10
THE 'MODERN' PHILLY MOB: JOSEPH LIGAMBI AND THE RETURN OF MERLINO

There is a saying that everything comes in three; a saying that, in context to the Philly Mob in the year 1999, rang exponentially true. In just under two decades, the organization had seen three massive law enforcement sting operations leading to the prosecutions of a large number of their members. It had been under the reign of three Bosses (if one counts the reign of 'Front Boss' Natale and underboss Merlino as one) who had destabilized the very structure of the Philly Mob. For another three, the third internal war within the organization, and the bloodiest yet, had also just ended, and the Philly Mob was once again left in a state of chaos. There is, however, one final act in the story, which is the history of the Philly Mob. After years under Bosses that brought the organization into the spotlight, along with all of its illicit activities and enterprises, leaving the Philly Mob vulnerable in the firing line of both law enforcement and the media, the time was now for a new Boss to enter the picture; a Boss that could douse the flames of a wrecked criminal family and move its operations back into the shadows. In this chapter, we will explore the reign of Joseph Ligambi, his ordering of a Philly Mob in disarray, the return of the flamboyant Merlino, and how the Philly Mob still holds sway in the modern age.

Joseph Ligambi

Joseph Anthony 'Uncle Joe' Ligambi was born in 1939. One of four children of Italian immigrants, his father worked as a cab driver in Philadelphia, where Ligambi went to school before dropping out in his junior year to join the United States Air Force. It has become a pattern in this exploration for those individuals we cover to have early lives rife with criminality and violence, but in Ligambi's case, this is not his story. In fact, Ligambi's first entry into criminality did not materialize until he was 32, when he was arrested for smuggling cigarettes. He worked as a bartender in the 1970s at a bar that was frequented by mobsters, leading to his association with brothers Lawrence 'Yogi' Merlino and Salvatore Merlino, who would become a *capo* and underboss under Scarfo's Philly Mob. Salvatore Merlino was also the father of future Boss Joseph Merlino. This is where Ligambi's connection and standing with the Philly Mob began to develop, as Salvatore Merlino took Ligambi under his wing, with Ligambi becoming his protege. Salvatore Merlino was close with Nicodemo Scarfo, who would take control of the family in 1981.

Now an associate of the Philly Mob and being mentored by a notable member of high repute, Ligambi began helping run illegal bookmaking operations for Salvatore and made money in the process, earning a reputation for his skill in sports handicapping (especially for football). In 1981, Scarfo became Boss of the Philly Mob, and Salvatore was appointed as underboss, further strengthening Ligambi's connections to the upper echelon of the organization. Ligambi even became a 'made man' of the Philly Mob in 1986, at the age of 47. This connection to the top came with a price, however. In 1985, Scarfo ordered a hit on Frank 'Frankie Flowers' D'Alfonso, a Philly Mob associate who had already been beaten by Scarfo's men for not paying Scarfo's 'street tax.' When two family members, Thomas DelGiorno and Eugene Milano, became government informants, they testified in court that Ligambi and Philip Narducci were the gunmen and Frank Narducci was the driver in the murder. DelGiorno and Milano had been part of the planning of the murder, along with Salvatore Merlino and Francis 'Faffy' Iannarella, hence their turn as government informants. In 1987, Ligambi was arrested for his role in D'Alfonso's murder. In April of 1989, Ligambi, Salvatore Merlino, Nicodemo Scarfo, Francis Iannarella, and the Narducci brothers were convicted of the murder and all handed life sentences.

This could have ended Ligambi there and then, fated to fade away in prison for the rest of his life. However, in 1992, Ligambi's luck changed. A court panel overturned his murder conviction, citing misconduct from the prosecution and trial-court errors. In 1997, a retrial was finally held, and Ligambi was acquitted of the murder. When Ligambi was released from prison in 1997, the Philly Mob was in the Natale-Merlino era (Natale as the 'Front Boss' and Merlino as the underboss). Ligambi came back to yet another Philly Mob that he had connections with. Underboss and the one truly pulling the strings of the organization, Joseph Merlino was the son of Ligambi's former mentor Salvatore Merlino. Also, *consigliere* George Borgesi, who had conspired and fought on the side of

Merlino during the Third Philadelphia Mafia War, was Ligambi's nephew. Still, Ligambi did not have much time to get used to this new hierarchy. In 1999, Merlino, Borgesi, and many other Merlino faction members were arrested, and it was Ligambi who was chosen to rule the Philly Mob as acting Boss while Merlino was in prison.

A Period of Stability

Ligambi inherited a Philly Mob that needed decisive leadership, having been decimated by years of chaos, conflict, and shifting hierarchy. Indeed, "history indicates that the job of Philly Mob Boss leads to a jail cell or a coffin. Of the six mob Bosses who preceded Ligambi, two were brutally murdered, and the other four ended up serving long prison sentences" (Scarpo, 2014). Ligambi had in front of him a Philly Mob that was still wounded from the Third Philadelphia Mafia War, with the divide created during the conflict still feeling very present. Ligambi's family members were a mix of older generation mobsters from the Scarfo and Stanfa eras and younger generation mobsters who supported Merlino's 'Young Turks.' "The volatility for which the Philadelphia crime family was once well known can return as swiftly as the time it takes to pull a trigger," so whatever Ligambi was planning to do, it had to entice and appease both factions (Scarpo, 2014). Ligambi managed to do much more than just that, with him not only gaining respect, "ironically from both law enforcement and the Five Families," for stabilizing the Philly Mob but also unifying the organization's two factions, managing to "rivet these two enclaves together" to form a new efficient and strong Philly Mob (Scarpo, 2014).

When Ligambi took over as acting Boss, he cleaned up the mess before him. Firstly, he dismantled the idea of a Philly Mob Boss being explicit, loud, and in the limelight that had become a trend in previous years. Ligambi took a less aggressive approach to running the organization, rarely being mentioned in the media, and overseeing operations from the shadows. When picking his inner circle, Ligambi appointed long-time Philadelphia mobsters Joseph 'Mousie' Massimino, Gaeton Lucibello, and Anthony Staino and began to rebuild relationships that had been shattered by Joseph Merlino's flamboyance and arrogance. Ligambi repaired the Philly Mob's relations with bookmakers, whom Merlino would make huge bets with and refuse to pay them off, and a whole host of criminal organizations (both national and local), who were put off working with the Philly Mob due to Merlino's brash, aggressive, and arrogant nature. Also, during Ligambi's reign, a fair amount of 'made men' were released from prison, many of whom were young members swallowed up by the Philly Mob's unstable history and were leaving prison older and wiser. Ligambi welcomed them back and put them to work. In 2004, Ligambi made Anthony Staino his underboss, with Staino reportedly being Ligambi's closest and most trusted ally. Under Ligambi, the Philly Mob also muscled in on a new, more modern enterprise: video poker. The organization took control of several video poker gambling machine businesses within Philadelphia.

Ligambi was bringing the Philly Mob back into business, molding it into an efficient criminal machine that did not attract too much attention. That being said, one can only be so quiet when running criminal enterprises, and in 2007, law enforcement took notice.

That year, 23 people, including four members of the Philly Mob, were charged with running an illegal sports betting operation out of a poker room at the Borgata Casino in Atlantic City. Ran by the Philly Mob, this operation brought in $60 million in bets, of which the Philly Mob kept the majority of the profits. Most individuals charged pleaded guilty, receiving sentences ranging from probation to five years. Law enforcement did also catch up with Ligambi, although not quite as successfully as they might have hoped. In May 2011, the FBI indicted Ligambi and 14 other Philly Mob members and associates on racketeering charges relating to illegal gambling operations, video poker gambling machines, and loan sharking. Seven of those members indicted plead guilty to lesser charges, with one becoming a government witness. However, the authorities had a harder time getting a charge to stick with Ligambi. Two years later, in 2013, two of the charges were dismissed against him. In 2014, Ligambi and his nephew and co-defendant George Borgesi were acquitted and released. Just like that, Ligambi had "beaten the feds twice in a case that has landed 10 of his associates in jail" (Scarpo, 2014). By keeping relative peace, Ligambi managed to revive a dying Philly Mob. Still, "peace should not be mistaken for weakness," with there being three major murders unsolved that occurred during Ligambi's tenure: Ronnie Turci in 1999, Raymond 'Long John' Martorano in 2002, and John 'Johnny Gongs' Casosanta in 2004. There are only scraps of evidence in these murders, and the authorities have yet to piece together anything resembling a case against Ligambi for them. While quiet and peaceful, Ligambi was still a mob Boss and did what the job required.

Merlino's Return

While Ligambi was rebuilding the Philly Mob, Merlino served his prison sentence at the Federal Correctional Institution of Terre Haute, Indiana. In March of 2011, after serving almost 12 years of his sentence, he was transferred to a halfway house in Florida, where he was to be on supervised release for three years. Just before his supervised release was to expire at the beginning of 2015, Merlino was handed a four-month sentence for violating the terms of the said supervised release by meeting with organized crime figures in Florida. In April of the same year, Merlino was released from the Federal Detention Center in Miami after his sentence was vacated, released ten days early after he won an appeal. In 2014, after being acquitted of racketeering charges, Ligambi stepped down as acting Boss due to the release of Merlino, who allegedly took his place as Boss of the Philly Mob, although Merlino himself denies this.

The 'organized crime figure' that Merlino had met during his parole in Florida was Nicholas 'Nicky Skins' Stefanelli, a soldier in the Gambino crime family. Stefanelli met with Merlino in 2011 to discuss numerous business ventures and projects, the nature and legality of which remain unclear. Merlino, who was "looking for a fresh start in Florida," was eager to hear him out (Anastasia, 2013). The start of the conversation went as expected, with Stefanelli focusing on the setting up of bars and restaurants, a venture he knew Merlino was interested in. However, Stefanelli had an altogether different agenda. He was wearing a wire and tasked with getting Merlino to talk about his involvement, past and present, with the Philly Mob. Stefanelli began to steer the conversation towards pending criminal cases of organized crime figures, including that of acting Boss Ligambi. Merlino made sure his answers were vague so as not to give anything that could be twisted against him, saying, "I said he was a nice guy, and I hoped he beats the case" (Anastasia, 2013). Stefanelli then asked about Nicky Jr., who was in federal prison awaiting trial on charges of extorting over $12 million from a mortgage company, with one of his co-conspirators being his father, Nicodemo Scarfo, 82 years of age and behind bars at the time. Again, Merlino spoke neutrally, recalling, "when he asked me about Scarfo, I said it was a shame what happened to that kid. I said his father was gonna get him 100 years, and I meant it" (Anastasia, 2013). A year later, Merlino learned of Stefanelli's wiring by authorities, stating, "the feds sent him down here to set me up. I told him I'm legitimate. I don't want nothing to do with any of that other stuff" (Anastasia, 2013). While Merlino continues to claim that he has nothing more to do with the Philly Mob and organized crime in general, the authorities seem to be having a hard time believing him. Indeed, they sent an informant to dig up dirt on him before he was even technically a free man. But Merlino proved in his conversation with Stefanelli "that he is savvy enough to know what to say and how to say it" (Anastasia, 2013).

In 2014, Merlino opened a restaurant in Boca Raton, Florida, named *Merlino's*, which has a menu filled with his mother's recipes. The establishment is owned by a group of investors as, due to his criminal record, Merlino is forbidden from owning an establishment that serves alcohol. As opposed to owning the restaurant, Merlino worked there officially as the head waiter until its closure in 2016. Regardless of Merlino's position on his involvement in criminal activities, trouble with law enforcement and other authorities manages to keep finding him. In 2016, the Pennsylvania Gaming Control Board banned Merlino from all casinos in Pennsylvania. In the same year, Merlino was arrested along with 45 others in a Racketeer Influenced and Corrupt Organizations (RICO) indictment. Detained at his home in Florida and brought to New York City for the trial, Merlino was charged with one count of racketeering, one count of fraud, and two counts of illegal gambling.

According to authorities, Merlino and the Genovese crime family had entered into illegal business arrangements. Merlino was also accused of participating in an insurance fraud scheme in Florida that involved doctors prescribing patients with unnecessary medication and billing their insurance companies. Later in the month of his arrest, Merlino was released on a $5 million bond. All other 45 individuals charged accepted plea deals, but not Merlino, who refused any plea deals and went to trial in January of 2018. After two weeks of testimony, a mistrial was declared after the jury could not come to a unanimous decision on any counts against Merlino. To obtain leverage and avoid a retrial, Merlino entered into a plea deal, agreeing to plead guilty to one minor charge in exchange for all other charges being dropped and a recommendation for a short sentence. In October of the same year, Merlino was sentenced to a maximum of two years in prison.

After a year, he was released early and served the rest of his sentence at a halfway house. A short time after, he was granted supervised release in South Florida. Merlino last appeared in the news in January 2023, when he was pictured with former United States

President Donald Trump at a Trump-owned golf course. In recent times, Trump has faced criticism for certain individuals he has been photographed with (including white supremacist political commentator Nick Fuentes) and has supposedly introduced improved vetting protocols to combat the criticism. In the case of Merlino, the Trump campaign brushed off the photograph, stating, "President Trump takes countless photos with people. That does not mean he knows every single person he comes in contact with" (Dorn, 2023). His relationship with Merlino aside, the last time Trump and the Philly Mob were linked so openly was way back in the 1980s Scarfo era, when many Trump-owned hotels and casinos were built during the resurgence of Atlantic City. A tenuous link perhaps, and indeed one that may bear no deeper meaning. But an interesting observation nonetheless. So, whether Merlino is the current Boss of the Philly Mob, and indeed whether he is involved in any organized crime at all, is a matter for debate. But, as Merlino says himself, "I was found not guilty. What else can I say?" (Anastasia, 2013).

The Philly Mob Today

Law enforcement, the FBI, and organized crime reporters all believe that, since Merlino's release from prison in 2011, he has continued to run the Philly Mob as Boss, with court documents from 2020 suggesting that, after stepping down as acting Boss, Joseph Ligambi now serves as Merlino's *consigliere*. The current underboss of the organization is Stephen Mazzone, who is presently in prison for illegal gambling, extortion, and loan sharking. Merlino, as we have seen, vehemently denies any involvement in the Philly Mob, citing his want to start an 'honest' life and his residence in Florida as proof of this, along with law enforcement's inability to prove any criminal activity. It is clear that if the Philly Mob is still actively operating (and it seems quite likely that they are), then they are doing it quietly, with many experts suggesting that they still maintain a stranglehold of power, influence, and stability, remaining to be one of the most active and powerful crime organizations in the United States. In 2016, it was reported that the Philly Mob had moved in on new business, with many members linked to the lucrative construction industry. In April 2018, four men made up of members and associates of the Philly Mob were arrested on drug trafficking charges in New Jersey, accused of distributing and selling large quantities of methamphetamine, heroin, fentanyl, and marijuana. The four accused pleaded guilty and received sentences between 5 and 15 years. In 2020, 15 members and associates of the Philly Mob were indicted on federal racketeering charges, amongst them being underboss Stephen Mazzone and *capo* Domenic Grande. The charges are somewhat classic for the organization: loan sharking, drug trafficking, and extortion.

CONCLUSION

The approximately 104-year history of the Philly Mob is one filled with many things: power, greed, violence, subterfuge, and death, to name but a few. Through this exploration, you have been taken on a journey through the creation, maintenance, destruction, and rebuilding of one of the most intriguing, dramatic, and successful organized crime families to have ever existed. Seen the rise and fall of 12 Bosses who, through their wildly varying styles of leadership and personalities, held the Philly Mob high above its contemporaries in the criminal underworld and also drove it so deep into the ground that it almost could not get back out again. Lived through three brutal civil wars for control of the organization as factions warred in bloody battles for domination, leaving nothing but rubble and bodies in their wake. Felt the constant friction between the law and the underworld, infinitely dueling in a game of cat and mouse. And witnessed the dark intermingling of loyalty and betrayal and how one must know which choice will keep you alive the longest.

Ultimately, the individuals that find themselves operating under the banner of organized crime are doing so for a variety of reasons. They are there to make a living, to earn power and respect, to carve out a life for themselves, but perhaps most potently, they are there to find purpose, to be part of something greater than themselves, and to find a family. It is this human aspect of organized crime that we generally tend to forget, brushing over it in search of the more dramatic aspects that come with operating within an organized crime family.

The fictionalized versions of gangsters from movies and television, like the examples of which that are given at the beginning of this book, tend to lean on the side of glorification; they portray the gangster as the wisecracker, the underdog, even arguably the hero, and there is nothing inherently wrong with this. It is perfectly acceptable to root for the gangster, and no doubt should be cast on this fact. If one takes anything away from this exploration into the history of the Philly Mob, it perhaps could be that organized crime, while wholly within the public eye on the screen and in books in a fictional capacity, has been and still is a very real entity with very real power and very real consequences. Also, to keep in one's mind that those who make up the muscle of the Philly Mob are, despite anything else, human. As we have seen time and time again, organized crime can bounce back from devastating circumstances, and consequently, it is quite reasonable to assume that the Philly Mob, and the individuals that are associated with it, can and will do the same, holding influence and power over many aspects of our modern society as they have done throughout history.

That being said, it feels rather prevalent to end this how we started, with a quote that encapsulates the very nature of organized crime:

Wherever there is opportunity, the Mafia will be there. –Johnny Kelley

REFERENCES

Anastasia, G. (2013, April 12). *Skinny Joey Talks About Nicky Skins And Life Without The Mob*. Big Trial | Philadelphia Trial Blog. https://www.bigtrial.net/2013/04/merlino-talks-about-nicky-skins-and.html

Anastasia, G., & Sausser, L. (2017, August 29). *Ron Previte, the Former Mobster who Brought Down Three Crime Bosses, Dies at 73*. PhillyVoice. https://www.phillyvoice.com/ron-previte-former-mobster-who-brought-down-three-crime-bosses-dies-73/

AZ Quotes. (2023). *Johnny Kelly Quote*. A-Z Quotes. https://www.azquotes.com/quote/773987

Behar, R., & Caramandi, N. (1991, June 17). *A Crow Turns Stool Pigeon: Nicholas Caramandi*. Time Magazine. https://content.time.com/time/subscriber/article/0,33009,973168,00.html

Burnstein, S. M., Cassidy, K., McShane, L., & Pearson, D. (2021, February 18). *The Mafia Boss who Flipped*. The Mob Museum. https://themobmuseum.org/blog/the-mafia-boss-who-flipped/

CBS News. (2013, March 17). *Hit man: Has a Mobster Found Redemption?* https://www.cbsnews.com/news/hit-man-has-a-mobster-found-redemption/

Chase, D. (Executive Producer). (1999, January 10). *The Sopranos* [TV series]. HBO.

Cipriano, R. (2010, October 29). *John-John Veasey's Life After the Philly Mob*. Philadelphia Magazine. https://www.phillymag.com/news/2010/10/29/john-john-veaseys-life-after-the-philly-mob/3/

Coppola, F. F. (Director). (1972, March 24). *The Godfather* [Film]. Paramount Pictures.

Dorn, S. (2023, January 23). *Trump Reportedly Pictured With Convicted Ex-Philly Mob Boss At Florida Golf Club*. Forbes. https://www.forbes.com/sites/saradorn/2023/01/23/trump-reportedly-pictured-with-convicted-ex-philly-mob-boss-at-florida-golf-club/

Dunn, M. (2021, August 18). *How The Apalachin Meeting Nearly Brought Down The Mafia*. All That's Interesting. https://allthatsinteresting.com/apalachin-meeting

Finkel, K. (2014, April 7). *Zanghi's Revenge: A Pivotal Mobster Moment – PhillyHistory Blog*. PhillyHistory Blog. https://blog.phillyhistory.org/index.php/2014/04/zanghis-revenge-a-pivotal-mobster-moment/

Helgeland, B. (Director). (2015, September 9). *Legend* [Film]. Studio Canal.

Hunt, T. (2021a). *Avena, John "Big Nose" (1893-1936)*. The American Mafia - Who Was Who. http://mob-who.blogspot.com/2011/04/avena-john-big-nose-1893-1936.html

Hunt, T. (2021). *Bruno, Joseph "Dovi" (1889-1946)*. The American Mafia - Who Was Who. http://mob-who.blogspot.com/2011/04/bruno-joseph-dovi-1889-1946.html

Hunt, T. P. (2023). *Philadelphia Crime Family Bosses*. American Mafia History. https://mafiahistory.us/maf-b-ph.html

Leonetti, P., & Graziano, C. (2014). *Mafia Prince: Inside America's Most Violent Crime Family and the Bloody Fall of La Cosa Nostra*. Running Press.

Long, B. (2020, February 14). *Remembering Philly and the Chicken Man*. The Northside Sun. http://northsidesun.com/news-columns-breaking-news/remembering-philly-and-chicken-man#sthash.NgIkeDQV.dpbs

Margaritoff, M. (2022, October 24). *He Led A Mafia Family For 35 Years, Then Wrote A Tell-All Book About It — And Somehow Lived To Tell The Tale*. All That's Interesting. https://allthatsinteresting.com/joe-bonanno

McKennett, H. (2019, November 4). *Angelo Bruno: The 'Docile Don' Who May Have Been Behind Hoffa's Death*. All That's Interesting. https://allthatsinteresting.com/angelo-bruno

Morello, C. A. (1999). *Before Bruno: 1880-1931* (Vol. 1). Celeste A. Morello.

Morello, C. A. (2005). *Before Bruno & How He Became Boss: The History of The Philadelphia Mafia Book Three: 1946-1959* (Vol. 3). Celeste A. Morello.

Notable Name: Vito Genovese. (2015). The Mob Museum. https://themobmuseum.org/notable_names/vito-genovese/

Patmore, N. (2022, August 4). '*A Greedy, Small-Minded, And Violent Terrorist': The Bloody Story Of 1980s Mob Boss Nicky Scarfo*. All That's Interesting. https://allthatsinteresting.com/nicky-scarfo

Pearson, D., & McShane, L. (2017). *Last Don Standing: The Secret Life of Mob Boss Ralph Natale*. St. Martin's Publishing Group.

Petepiece, A. (2018). *The Mafia Commission: A History of the Board of Directors of La Cosa Nostra*. Tellwell Talent.

Press, T. A. (2001, December 4). National Briefing | Mid-Atlantic: Pennsylvania: Mobster Gets 14 Years (Published 2001). *The New York Times*. https://www.nytimes.com/2001/12/04/us/national-briefing-mid-atlantic-pennsylvania-mobster-gets-14-years.html

Raab, S. (1995, October 6). Brother of Mob Turncoat Is Gunned Down. *The New York Times*. https://www.nytimes.com/1995/10/06/us/brother-of-mob-turncoat-is-gunned-down.html

Roberts, S. (2017, January 17). Nicky Scarfo, Mob Boss Who Plundered Atlantic City in the '80s, Dies at 87 (Published 2017). *The New York Times*. https://www.nytimes.com/2017/01/17/nyregion/nicky-scarfo-mob-boss-who-plundered-atlantic-city-in-the-80s-dies-at-87.html

Roebuck, J. (2017, August 29). *Ron Previte, wiseguy informant who brought down Philly mob bosses, dead at 73*. Https://Www.inquirer.com. https://www.inquirer.com/philly/obituaries/ron-previte-dies-informant-mob-bosses-philly-20170829.html

Scarpo, E. (17, July 2014). *If Uncle Joe Retires What Happens in Philadelphia?* Cosa Nostra News. https://www.cosanostranews.com/2014/03/philly-mob-boss-uncle-joe-says-hes-done.html

Scorsese, M. (Director). (2019, November 1). *The Irishman* [Film]. Netflix.

Springsteen, B. (1982). *Atlantic City*. YouTube. https://www.youtube.com/watch?v=M3eu1gW-bQ8

Winter, T. (Executive Producer). (2010, September 19). *Boardwalk Empire* [TV series]. HBO.

THE DECAVALCANTE MAFIA CRIME FAMILY

INTRODUCTION

As you make your way down the New Jersey Turnpike, the gritty landscape of the Garden State unfolds before you. The green-painted overpasses and bridges flash by, a blur of concrete and steel. You pass by shuttered factories and warehouses, their broken windows staring out at you like empty eyes. Just ahead, you can see the Meadowlands, a vast expanse of swampland that stretches out to the horizon.

As the distinct perfume of this part of the New York metropolitan area wafts through the air, your nostrils are singed by the spoiled-cheese fog that emanates from waste disposal plants and rendering facilities and the sulphuric mixture of pollution that leaks from every nook and cranny of the industrial zones of Elizabeth and Newark.

As New Jersey's "signature fragrance" suspends itself in a greenish-gray plume above you, you look off into the distance and see that it stretches all the way across the Goethals Bridge and deep into Staten Island, where it lingers above the Arthur Kill, joining hands with the malodorous expulsions that drift northward from the Fresh Kills Landfill.

Driving through the Meadowlands in your 1982 Cadillac DeVille, fitted with leather upholstery and whitewall tires with platinumspoked wheel covers and curb feelers, you know that there are all kinds of secrets buried in those murky swamps—secrets that would shock the average person. But you're no average person. You're a made guy in the DeCavalcante family, the oldest crime family to operate on this side of the river, a soldier operating within the dark underbelly of society, where violence, money, and power come before all else.

You turn off the highway and onto a narrow side street, the sound of your tires echoing off the crumbling buildings. This is the heart of old-school Italian–American New Jersey, a place where your associates' pizza shops and pork stores sit alongside mom-and-pop delis, bakeries, and five and dimes. As you creep by in the Caddy, you cast a knowing glare and nod over to your uncle, or as the *paisani* say, Zio Ciccio, the old man who still makes his own wine in his basement and is still out on the stoop, espresso cup in hand every morning.

You think back to what it was like growing up on these streets. This was your block, where you grew up, where you devoured plate after plate of Mom's ziti, where you had your first communion; this is the place where you pinched your first wallet, made your first collection, and learned how to fight; it's the place where you learned the ropes of "our thing." Being a made guy isn't all fun and games, though. It's all about the hustle, all about making sure the Family's interests are protected. That means collecting debts, settling disputes, and taking care of any problems that might arise. It's a tough job, but it's the only life you've ever known.

As you pull up to your destination, you can't help but wonder what the future holds. Will you be able to make your way up the ranks, or will you be stuck in a life of low-level errands like this one forever? Only time will tell. As you approach the venue of the private poker club, the smell of cigarettes and sweat fills the air. You can hear the sound of chips clinking and the low murmur of voices from inside.

You take a deep breath and push open the door, your hand instinctively drifting to the gun hidden in your waistband. The room falls silent as you make your way through the crowd, your eyes fixed on the man you've come to see. He's a small-time hustler with a reputation for racking up debts, but you know better than to underestimate him. He's got connections all over the city, and you can't afford to make an enemy of him.

You approach the table with a cool confidence, your every step measured and calculated. "I'm here to collect," you say, your voice low and steady. The man sneers up at you, his eyes bleary from a few too many neat whiskies down the gullet. "You can't be serious," he spits out, slamming his fists on the table. "You know I don't have that kind of cash on hand."

You can feel the tension in the room rising, and you know you have to act fast. You pull out your gun and rap the table with it, sending chips and cards flying, the metal ringing out in the silence. As you calmly take aim directly at his insolent, thick skull, you mutter, "You've got until the count of ten to come up with the money." You tone your voice down a scale. "Or things are going to get ugly."

The man's eyes widen in fear, and he starts to beg for mercy. But you've heard it all before, and you know there's no backing down now. You start to count, the seconds ticking by like hours. Just as you reach nine, the man extends his arm straight up in a gesture of surrender, a wad of cash that, conveniently, he "didn't have" before now clutched between his fingertips.

You snatch it up and pocket it, your mission accomplished. As you walk out of the poker room, the adrenaline is still pumping through your veins. You know that this is just one small piece of the puzzle, that there are always more debts to collect and more rivals to take down. But in this world of violence, money, and power, you wouldn't have it any other way. You are a DeCavalcante family soldier, and this is just another day in the life of a made guy.

As you get back into your car, you think to yourself, and can't help but wonder, *Marron! How did I end up doin' this shit?* To find out, we'll have to go back to the beginning, to the roots of organized crime in New Jersey, and how the family that would come to be known as DeCavalcante got their start.

CHAPTER 1
FAMILY HISTORY

The Peterstown section of Elizabeth, New Jersey is an unassuming-enough area, its streets dotted with well-kept apartment buildings and modest single- and multi-family homes: a peaceful immigrant enclave, where every decade or so sees the next wave of inhabitants coming in to replace the last one, as their modest, blue-collar jobs and frugal, community-oriented approach to life allows residents to send their kids off to college and move out of this bustling urban neighborhood, out to more affluent suburbs.

While the current-day mix in Peterstown is now heavily Latino, once upon a time this neighborhood was home to a vibrant Italian–American community, the remnants of which can still be seen around the blocks that still bear the evidence of this time.

At 408 Palmer Street lies the Ribera Social Club, a brick-face, white-columned event and function hall that's open to public bookings for all kinds of celebrations, from weddings to baby showers to quinceañeras. While this unassuming structure seems just like any other social club or fraternal organization—as are common in urban communities like Elizabeth—this one happens to be home to the most notorious criminal organization in the entire state.

With deep ties to the Agrigento province of Sicily that remain in place to this day, the Ribera Club still actively recruits members from Italy to come over to do "jobs," including but not limited to racketeering, drug trafficking, illegal gambling, loansharking, money laundering, extortion, murder, construction and job site violations, fraud, and larceny (Garrett T., 2009).

Although the pool of overseas recruits who come directly from the old country has decreased significantly in recent years, the DeCavalcante family endures, actively recruiting guys from New York, New Jersey, and Philadelphia, in addition to some from Sicily. Maintaining active connections with several other organizations, most notably the Five Families of New York and Philadelphia's Bruno–Scarfo crime family, the DeCavalcante family has been in existence since the early 1900s and is not only recognized as one of the oldest Mafia families in the entire country but also carries the honor of being the only "born-and-bred" New Jersey family of La Cosa Nostra (LCN).

While the powerful New York families have always had a hand in what went on across the Hudson, the DeCavalcante family has continued to hold things down on their home turf throughout their history. Though often referred to by their more sophisticated New York counterparts as "farmers," the DeCavalcante family today are anything but, their ranks filled with modern-day, blue-collar workers and aspirational middle-class types—not the kind of backwoods country boys that the name implies. It's believed that this term originated only from the fact that the DeCavalcante family acted as a "farm team" for many years, giving guys some experience before making it up to the "big leagues" of the larger, more powerful

New York families. There's also a possibility that this slightly derogatory name is derived from New Jersey's history in agricultural production: Today the Garden State is still an important grower of tomatoes and other crops.

Despite sometimes garnering condescending downtalk, and being viewed overall as less powerful and sophisticated than the New York families, the DeCavalcante family's smaller size has made them agile and able to evade law enforcement in many instances throughout their history. Often including just 35–50 made guys at any given time (though the numbers can vary due to prison sentences, "disappearances," etc.), the organization has also consistently relied on an ever-changing extended circle of up to 100 criminal associates, making both their ranks and extended network rather tight compared to those of larger families.

The story of how the DeCavalcante family came to become New Jersey's original crime family traces its origins back to Sicily, specifically Ribera, the Italian municipality, or *comune*, which lends its name to the club at 408 Palmer. It all started with a man named Stefano Badami, who made his passage to America sometime during the mid to late 1920s.

Family Origins: The Elizabeth and Newark Families

Born on December 10, 1888, in Corleone, Sicily, and baptized the following day, it's unknown when Badami first came to the United States, though immigration records point to a possibility that he may have entered the country not directly from Italy but, rather, through the Canadian border. What is known about Badami's early years and personal life is that he married Giuseppa Gugliatta on

October 26, 1924, in Roccamena, Sicily, and that when he first came to America, he settled in Newark, where records show he opened a clothing factory.

Garment manufacturing in New York and New Jersey was an important industry at the time. If, as records show, Badami was able to open a factory shortly after arriving in America, he must have already had a solid financial base or some kind of backing, likely from his connections back in Sicily. Though the records on the details of Badami's early career and business interests are nonexistent, it's possible that he could have been delegated this role of factory "owner" by a higher-up.

That said, since Badami would have been in his mid-30s by the time he moved to America, he may have already amassed a personal fortune through his business dealings back in Sicily, making it possible that he already had the financial resources himself to open a factory. The way in which this factory venture was financed, and whether that money was obtained through legal or illegal means, remains unclear.

At the time that Badami arrived in America, most Sicilian immigrants were still at the bottom rung of the labor market. At the time, common jobs for recent arrivals included day labor in the construction industry, jobs down at the docks, or other forms of back-breaking physical work. When Sicilians first came to the country in the mid-1800s, they took agricultural jobs that were recently vacated by newly freed slaves. By the early 1900s, they were often employed as fruit vendors and street peddlers in large urban areas, such as in New York and New Jersey where they migrated, often sending for their wives and children once they had the money saved up to do so.

Sicilians had been coming to the US for some time already, but even after decades, they were still viewed as insular; they were stereotyped in print, as well as within the communities they moved into, as having tendencies toward criminality. One reason why these immigrants took a distrust of government and institutions with them to their adopted home was due to their experiences back in Italy with Garibaldi's economic reforms and push toward forming a republic, changes that left the entire southern part of the Italian Peninsula dirt poor and under the domination of the richer, more developed North. Widespread corruption in their home *comuni* often led them to be distrustful of law enforcement.

The likelihood that Badami already had money or a financial backer when he arrived suggests that he had some deep connections with some powerful groups or individuals back home. These connections and ties to Ribera, Sicily, and the Sicilian Mafia would come to play a big role once the United States became a dry country in 1920 after having passed the 18th amendment to the constitution the previous year.

Prohibition-era America saw rampant production of illegal alcoholic beverages, which brought on a spike in crime and all kinds of other illicit activity. The money in the illegal trafficking of booze was highly lucrative, so it makes sense that the Sicilian Mafia would want a piece of the pie. During the Prohibition years, Badami would become a key figure in the New Jersey Mafia with his gang based in Elizabeth, New Jersey.

The Newark and Elizabeth families would become the two main players in the bootlegging and racketeering that took place in New Jersey during the Prohibition years. At first, bootlegging operations in the city of Newark were split between the control of two families: Gaspare D'Amico's family, which would come to be called the Newark family, and the family of Stefano Badami, which would come to be called the Elizabeth family.

Bootlegging and Early Criminal Activities

D'Amico was based locally in Newark while Badami operated out of neighboring Elizabeth, and they managed to share the territory without too much trouble for some years. D'Amico was also known to oversee illegal gambling operations during the 1920s, and had a few other things going at the time, so the fact that there was outside interest in the lucrative trafficking of illicit booze within Newark city limits was likely not a main concern of his. In fact, there was already another mobster, Gaetano "Tom" Reina, who later became head of the Lucchese crime family, involved in the transportation of whiskey and other types of alcohol in North Jersey during Prohibition times.

In 1935, Vincenzo Troia, an associate of "boss of all bosses" Salvatore Maranzano, had plans to seize control of the Newark clan, but he was preemptively taken down before he could execute his plotted takeover of the Newark turf. Then, 2 years later, Giuseppe "Joe" Profaci, who would later go on to found the Colombo family, decided that he was going to take Newark's D'Amico down himself, in an attempt to seize the entire territory. After D'Amico was targeted in an assassination attempt that was orchestrated by

Profaci, he decided to flee the country, leaving the Newark turf up for grabs.

Once D'Amico was out of the picture, the higher-ups in the Commission, the governing body of LCN and the Five Families, which was founded by mobster Charles "Lucky" Luciano, voted to redistribute D'Amico's territory among New York's Five Families and Stefano Badami's Elizabeth crew. Strategically located in neighboring Elizabeth and already operating within Newark city limits, Badami had the mandate to dominate the area, using his alliance with the Five Families to fend off any potential outside threats. Badami would go on to find, however, that the majority of the threats he'd face would come from within his own ranks.

Despite being installed de facto by the Commission as leader of the newly pieced-together Elizabeth–Newark group, Badami was unable to bring about unity within the fledgling organization, as Newark crew members, who had previously been under D'Amico's command, and Badami's Elizabeth guys continuously fought with each other for dominance over different business interests across the overlapping territories. Badami's leadership would continue to be marked by this kind of intragroup conflict throughout his entire tenure, and he was eventually murdered in 1955 during what seems to have been a power struggle between warring members of the combined groups.

Trouble in Newark

Once D'Amico fled back to Sicily in 1937 and Badami was installed as leader of the joint Elizabeth–Newark family, a feud broke out. There are several theories as to the origins of the feud between the

Newark family and the Elizabeth family, though it seems to have started during the time that D'Amico was still running Newark.

Some have asserted that, under D'Amico's leadership, Newark had only inducted Sicilians into their crew and excluded Calabrians, pointing to a possibility that the internal conflict may have stemmed from this history of intragroup discrimination. Others have suggested that another source of tension could have been related to the supposedly unjustified killings of members of the Troia family in which D'Amico was implicated. Even though D'Amico had been a victim of Troia's takeover plot, which warranted retaliation, some thought he took things too far in targeting his enemies.

Aside from the brewing intragroup conflict that plagued the Elizabeth–Newark crew, there may have also been some lingering external threats stemming from some unwise decisions made on D'Amico's part in the period that preceded his departure. During his time as head of Newark, D'Amico may have instructed members of his faction to block Joe Profaci's truck routes in the olive oil distribution business that were crossing over into Newark territory.

In addition to this potential point of conflict, some say that D'Amico owed Profaci a large sum of money before the attempts on his life at the hand of Troia, which motivated him to hurriedly flee back to Sicily before making good on his debts. Also important to note is that D'Amico and Profaci often had different interests in turf battles and power struggles that played out among other Mafia families, and that they supported different sides in a power struggle back home in Profaci's native Villabate, a suburb of Palermo.

The tensions that had already existed between Profaci and D'Amico seemed to remain in his absence, even though Badami had already been installed as the new boss of the Elizabeth–Newark family. At the start of the Castellammarese War, both Badami and Profaci were said to be aligned with Maranzano, so it's not known whether this local mob conflict back in the old country played a significant role in the tensions between Profaci and the Elizabeth–Newark family.

While conflict over territory and power had been building up for some time already, the escalation of these tensions led to an outbreak in the ongoing war within the Elizabeth and Newark factions, and the arrival of the 1950s heralded a marked rise in violence, which built up like a pressure cooker until the point when Badami got whacked in 1955.

During this era of conflict, Joe Bonanno and Vincent Mangano supported the Elizabeth faction while Willie Moretti and Thomas Lucchese were in favor of the proposal that would eventually come to be realized: The entire Elizabeth–Newark family should be distributed among the other families (Vacari, 2021).

The Genovese, Gambino, Lucchese, and Profaci families all took on members from the Elizabeth–Newark crew during this time, cementing the group's reputation for being "farmable." Some members, such as Tony Caponigro, chose to join the Philadelphia crime family instead, due to their existing relationships with Joe Ida and Marco Reginelli.

The culmination of all this intracrew and external conflict that went on between the combined ranks of the Newark and Elizabeth factions came with Badami getting stabbed to death at Vito's Clam Bar in Newark in 1955 by Frank Monaco, the brother of Badami's former underboss, Sam Monaco.

Sam Monaco had "disappeared" back in 1931 in the aftermath of the Castellammarese War, on the same day that Charles "Lucky" Luciano's hit on "boss of all bosses" Salvatore Maranzano was carried out. Monaco and Luigi "Louis" Russo's remains were found a few days later floating in Newark Bay, somehow defying the gravity of the weights that had been attached to their bodies after being brutally tortured and executed.

Anyway, Badami was stabbed to death at the clam shack by old Frank, Sam's brother, on March 31, 1955, and while it's unknown whether razor clams were on the menu of daily specials, there were certainly blades of one kind or another flying around that day. It's likely that quite a mess was made, with blood and clamshells strewn about the bayside seafood shack and notable wiseguy hangout.

Once the rubble had settled after this period of conflict, the remnants of the two factions from Elizabeth and Newark would continue to mingle and coexist in a suspended state of constant conflict. There would still be many years of struggle and infighting ahead before they would eventually come together, forgetting the transgressions of the past to arise anew under the DeCavalcante name.

The First Bosses

While Stefano Badami's tenure as boss of the Elizabeth–Newark family is remembered for his inability to reconcile the conflicting power dynamics within the two merging crews, it's important to note that this era was defined largely by decisions made by the Commission and the roles played by other, larger crime families, such as Joe Profaci's. Aside from this aspect of examining Badami's reign, and lapses in history and records, there are a few details of Badami's life and involvement in organized crime that remain murky.

In addition to it not being clear exactly when he arrived in America, there are other details of his personal life and travels that leave holes in existing knowledge of his personal relationships and dealings. One example is that, while records state that he married Giuseppa Gugliatta on October 26, 1924, in Roccamena, Sicily, Badami was later wed to Mary Landusco Miele in 1953, listing "single" on the marriage license and indicating that somewhere along the line his first wife may have "disappeared."

Another piece of information, the details of which are not known, is Badami's connections with Canada—with some suggesting that he may have first entered the United States through the Canadian border. What is known according to public records is that he was twice denied entry to the country through its New York border in 1929.

While most Mafia historians agree that Badami was a high-ranking member of the Elizabeth–Newark Mafia, there is no agreement on whether or not he was actually capo, and details like his exact role within the organization and the time period in which he was in charge remain unconfirmed.

Also unclear are Badami's roles in the garment industry rackets and the specific details of his factory ownership. It is known, however, that the Mafia would later express a great interest in that industry, specifically in the business of trucking articles of clothing, so much so that it would become one of the key talking points at the Apalachin meeting in 1957.

Aside from any discrepancies or lapses in history, as expected in histories dating all the way back to the early 20th century, Badami is definitively named in most histories of the American Mafia as the Prohibition-era capo of the Elizabeth–Newark family and as the founder of what would eventually become the DeCavalcante family.

Stepping into the seat of power once Badami was out of the picture, underboss Filippo "Phil" Amari continued running the bootlegging operations of the Elizabeth–Newark crew and branched out into a range of other ventures, including extortion, racketeering, loansharking, and drug trafficking, both in Newark and New York City. He was seen as the new leader of the New Jersey crime organization, but his position was short lived, as there were still multiple factions within the group at war with each other. In response to this ongoing tumult, Amari chose to follow in the footsteps of former Newark boss Gaspare D'Amico and relocate back to Sicily. Amari was subsequently replaced by Nicholas "Nick" Delmore.

Dealings with the governing body of LCN and other larger, more formally organized crime groups would come to have a profound effect on the outcomes of what went down in Jersey going forward into the 20th century. Three key players of the Elizabeth–Newark crew would further cement the connections and dynamics of this fledgling Jersey group by attending the storied Apalachin meeting of 1957. Nicholas "Nick" Delmore and underbosses Francesco "Big Frank" Majuri and Louis "Fat Lou" LaRasso were all in attendance at this mob-world summit that made history for its bold attempt at bringing together Mafia members from all across the country, as well as for its quick snuffing-out and the mass arrests that took place in its wake.

Taking place in November 1957 at the upstate New York home of Joseph "Joe the Barber" Barbara, the Apalachin meeting was a notorious summit held between the families of the American Mafia that brought together nearly 100 LCN members to discuss all things crime related—that was, until an unexpected visit by a state trooper sent goombahs fleeing Barbara's estate.

The cop had been on patrol, noticed the presence of hundreds of late-model luxury cars with out-of-state license plates parked near the property, and knew that there was something suspicious going on. As soon as the heat rolled up, the crowd of wiseguys began to disperse, making their passage through the local woods.

Like the scene in Season 5 of *The Sopranos* when Tony makes his escape through the snowy woods from the FBI agents who so rudely interrupt his meeting with Johnny Sack outside the New York boss's mansion, wiseguys fleeing the Apalachin meeting were no doubt subject to the comical escapades that occur when mobsters are sent out into nature.

Take the "Pine Barrens" episode of *The Sopranos* for instance, in which Paulie Walnuts and Chris Moltisanti are challenged to the extreme as they try to navigate a botched mission deep in the woods of southern New Jersey. Paulie's always-dapper sartorial preferences make for some challenges as the two chase down a crazed Russian, who's somehow thwarted all their efforts to give him a proper burial by suddenly springing to life and leading the wiseguys on a wild-goose chase that ends with them nearly freezing to death as they await Tony's rescue.

As Paulie's wingtips and hand-tailored suit meet the rugged, unforgiving terrain of the American wilderness, it makes for a clear demonstration that these streetwise soldiers might be prepared to face all kinds of challenges in their home environment, but when confronted with nature, the tough exterior they present can easily crack. So, now that you've got these familiar images set in your head, let's get back to reality and talk about what went down on that day in 1957, the real-life event that informed these iconic TV moments.

The agenda for that day was supposed to be packed with discussions on a range of topics, including gambling, loansharking, trucking, and the drug trade. The territory and dealings of Umberto "Albert" Anastasia were also on the table, as his recent barbershop visit ended with him taking six bullets to the skull—talk about a close shave! The meeting was set to allow Vito Genovese (heir apparent to the Luciano family, which would later come to take Vito's own last name) to cement his newly inherited power by arranging a big summit that included mobbed-up guys from all over.

Some of the most prominent leaders of LCN—including Santo Trafficante Jr., Russell Bufalino of the Northeastern Pennsylvania family, Frank DeSimone of Los Angeles, Carlos "Little Man" Marcello, and Meyer Lansky—were in attendance because they harbored concerns about Anastasia's attempts at gaining control of their casino operations in Havana.

Another key topic on the agenda of the Apalachin meeting was the New York garment industry, an industry that, as already discussed, may have played a key role in Badami's early years. Discussion of this industry at the Apalachin meeting was to include both loansharking to business owners and control over trucking in New York's garment center. The outcome of these discussions would have an effect on the business interests of other bosses around the country, particularly those related to garment manufacturing, trucking, labor, and unions, all of which generated significant amounts of cash for the families that had a hand in these rackets.

The botched meeting ended in the arrest of both Frank Majuri and Louis LaRasso, underbosses of Elizabeth and Newark respectively, both of whom would remain key members in the DeCavalcante family. It is presumed that Nick Delmore made a successful Tony Soprano-like escape through the woods of Apalachin, New York, on that day, as he was not arrested.

Delmore's 2 underbosses, however, were not so lucky. Majuri and LaRasso were both charged with and found guilty of conspiracy. All of the 20 mafiosi charged and indicted following their arrests at the Apalachin meeting were fined up to $10,000 each and were sentenced to prison for 3–5 years (*The Blade*, 1960). All of these convictions, however, were overturned the following year, and these mobbed-up guys were soon back on the streets.

Delmore's time as leader of the Elizabeth–Newark family was characterized by the group's clandestine operations. The fact that the group was still not known to law enforcement was an advantage that was played smartly, as the clan's small size and low profile allowed them to continue their nefarious dealings. In fact, at the time of the Apalachin meeting, the Feds thought that Delmore and his crew were just underlings, members of a larger family or associations of the Genovese, the Gambinos, or Joseph "Joe" Profaci's crew (which would later go on to become the Colombo family).

Little did law enforcement know that they had an independent family on their hands. But they'd know soon enough, as the man who'd give the family their name would come to be the successor to leadership in just a few years. Delmore continued to lead the organization until his passing in 1964, leaving the reins of power to his nephew, Simone Rizzo DeCavalcante.

By the time DeCavalcante came in as the new boss of the family, lending his name to the group, a new era had begun. This change in leadership and priorities would set the stage for the future of organized crime in New Jersey and, for the first time, would gain this fledgling crew from Elizabeth and Newark official recognition by (though not a seat at the table of) the Commission—the governing body of the Italian–American Mafia.

Though Delmore, Majuri, and LaRasso's attendance at the Apalachin meeting signified that the Elizabeth–Newark family was already making inroads at becoming recognized as an autonomous and legitimate family within LCN, it wasn't until DeCavalcante entered the picture that the boys from Jersey really came into the fully realized and recognized form that would carry the family into the modern era.

Rise of "The Count": Simone DeCavalcante

When his uncle, Nicky Delmore, kicked the bucket in 1964, Simone Rizzo "Sam" DeCavalcante, aka "Sam the Plumber," aka "The Count," made quick moves to legitimize his grip on power and to boost his crew's standing with the Commission. A Trenton, New Jersey, native, who claimed to be descended from Italian royalty, was now heir apparent to the struggling local mob family that had somehow survived bootlegging crackdowns, multiple mob wars, and the risk of being swallowed up and farmed out by their larger New York counterparts.

For Sam's unverified assertion of royal lineage, he'd gain the nickname "The Count," but only once he came into his inheritance—the keys to a slightly dysfunctional crew of ex-bootleggers from Elizabeth and Newark—would he truly become the monarch he always believed himself to be.

CHAPTER 2
DECAVALCANTE

Sam The Plumber

Kenilworth Heating and Air Conditioning, a run-of-the-mill local business in the sleepy suburb of Kenilworth, New Jersey, was just like any number of other local businesses in the area. It responded to customers' needs, paid its taxes, and maybe even participated in some local business organizations. Most importantly, Kenilworth Heating and Air Conditioning fulfilled all of its civic and legal duties in the interest of providing useful services to the community. But there was one thing that set this service and maintenance company apart from many other local businesses: Its proprietor was Simone "Sam the Plumber" DeCavalcante.

Though DeCavalcante was incarcerated just five years after assuming control of his now namesake Mafia family, he managed to reorganize and legitimize the fledgling group he came into while also growing it, doubling the ranks of made guys under his command within just a few years of taking control. By showing he meant serious business to the other families around, he was able to define a path forward toward modernization with a series of reforms that would boost his mismatched and sometimes underappreciated crew of New Jersey "farmers" to previously unknown heights.

DeCavalcante's experience running a legitimate business may have helped him in establishing new ways of operating and in setting new goals and priorities for the family. Setting a precedent for future DeCavalcante bosses, some of whom would also skirt the gray area between legitimate and illegal businesses, he made profitability his number one focus while also managing to keep things settled within the ranks.

Aside from the inroads he made with the Commission and with maintaining good relations with other mafiosi across the region, DeCavalcante was able to raise the family's array of illegal income sources to the point where they had revenue of up to $20 million per year (*The New York Times*, 1971).

Another one of DeCavalcante's reforms increased the scope and reach of the operations, branching out further into New York City, as well as into other geographic areas, including Waterbury, Connecticut, where business dealings of a satellite crew were under the charge of underboss Joseph "Joe Buff" LaSelva. DeCavalcante was also successful in expanding their reach to Florida, where a number of other members and associates were installed.

At this time the main activities of the family included gambling, loansharking, union racketeering, extortion, and drug trafficking. DeCavalcante proved to be able to run his family efficiently and also managed to gain the respect of its members as well as satisfy the sometimes finicky demands and expectations of its New York Mafia connections.

Though DeCavalcante's assumption of power settled down many of the tensions and internal conflicts that had plagued the ranks of the Elizabeth–Newark crew since its bootlegging days, a new series of problems would take the group head-on, bringing some unforeseen challenges. Stemming from their newly raised profile and ranking within the greater world of New York City organized crime, the DeCavalcante family began to attract attention from law enforcement, something they had long avoided due to their small size and the muted status they previously held. This reality, met with a series of new efforts and initiatives by the FBI, made for a difficult period in which government surveillance began to creep in. Gone were the days when homegrown New Jersey organized crime could slip through the cracks, somewhat protected by the shadows cast by their high-profile, bigger New York counterparts.

He didn't know it at the time, but the FBI had DeCavalcante bugged from the get-go, when he took over upon his uncle's death in 1964. The bugs they placed in the office of Kenilworth Heating and Air Conditioning allowed the Feds to capture recordings of Sam the Plumber referring to his dealings with the Commission, revealing his associations with other crime families, and exposing his agenda. As they continued eavesdropping on his conversations, various other pieces of information tied to the illicit activity he was involved in began to emerge.

Aside from revealing the details of DeCavalcante's crimes and connections, the audio that the Feds captured revealed private details of the goombah plumber's life, including some very private information regarding the marital affairs he was involved in. The recordings also revealed some talk about his inner life, some of which seems straight out of *The Sopranos*. Like Tony, Sam the Plumber was racked with the same kind of heavy burdens and carried the psychological weight that any mob boss with some semblance of a conscience would be forced to endure.

Masterminding crimes and killing people for a living takes its toll, and the transcripts from the bugs planted inside the office of Kenilworth Heating and Air Conditioning reveal some insights into what it's like to struggle with the issues that any mob boss must confront and process. Like Tony's fever-dream sequences that begin in the last episode of Season 2—when he gets food poisoning after devouring an Indian dinner with Salvatore "Big Pussy" Bonpensiero, followed by a plate of mussels at Artie Bucco's—some of Sam's own dreams that were captured on tape reveal some of the same elements of symbolism that Tony's often do.

Describing a dream in which DeCavalcante was being pursued by the police and his secretary also appeared, he told her in one recording, "You were screaming… You had pearls on… Everything was so screwed up… Mary [his wife] woke me up… something about pearls… I don't remember" (Daly, 2017, para. 3). Possibly revealing Sam's guilt around the affair he was having with his secretary, the combined imagery of getting chased down by cops while his pearl-clutching *goomar* cries out points to the possibility that DeCavalcante feared getting caught in any of his multiple affairs.

Aside from DeCavalcante's personal transgressions, the details of crimes committed that were also revealed in the audio tape were enough to bring charges of racketeering against him, and in 1969, he was convicted of these charges and sent away to prison. Upon being released in 1976, DeCavalcante went into "retirement" in Florida, although a 2004 report on organized crime carried out by the State of New Jersey maintains that DeCavalcante continued to serve as boss of his namesake clan up until 1982 (Commission of Investigation) when the next boss would assume control of the DeCavalcante family.

During DeCavalcante's exile in the Sunshine State, the guy who would eventually take over from Sam the Plumber was rising up the ranks. This detailed-oriented and well-respected underboss's name was John Riggi. A "well-groomed" guy whose father, Emmanuel Riggi, had long served the family as an agent operating within various labor unions, John Riggi also had deep connections of his own within this important part of the DeCavalcante business. Making inroads by leveraging his influence within the unions, he was well poised to assume the position of family boss ("DeCavalcante Family," 2022).

Riggi's Way: John "The Eagle" Riggi

Like DeCavalcante before him, John "The Eagle" Riggi was a straightforward guy who had the respect of the Five Families, maintaining good relations with the larger powers at hand throughout the region. Riggi continued to spread the sails of the family's boosted profile and their higher standing within LCN that Sam DeCavalcante put into motion, and he even had a close personal relationship with the boss of the Gambino family, John Gotti.

Riggi decided that, for the first time, a ruling panel would be incorporated into the DeCavalcante leadership structure, and that it would be run by Gaetano "Corky" Vastola. Vastola, an old-time mobster, had dealings in the entertainment industry that have drawn comparisons to *The Sopranos* character Hesh Rabkin, Tony's Jewish consigliere, who made his fortune as founder of the fictional F-Note Records. As the head of Roulette Records, Vastola was known to hang out with Sammy Davis Jr. and had also worked as a concert promoter.

Riggi was thought of by the ruling panel and the underlings further downstream in the ranks as an even-tempered leader who ruled with an iron fist, capable of ordering hits on enemies without batting an eyelash, and sometimes even carrying them out himself. He was both feared and respected, setting him up for a continued trajectory toward maintaining the stability that was achieved by his predecessor.

Taking things from where Sam the Plumber left off, Riggi maintained similar standards for conduct in business and mob relations and was known for his management skills, which would continue to support the array of illicit activities that DeCavalcante had pulled together during his reign while also adding some more in Riggi's own areas of expertise.

Once Riggi took over, the most lucrative sources of revenue for the family were gambling and loansharking, but there were a number of other rackets that came to be important during his tenure. Labor racketeering was one of the areas that Riggi excelled at, and in expanding and introducing new sources of revenue through linking up with local labor unions and contractors, he ensured that activities in the area would continue to be an important part of the family's crime portfolio throughout the latter half of the 20th century and into the 21st.

Riggi's focus on union activity gave him a huge advantage within the construction, municipal projects, and transportation industries, and like DeCavalcante before him, Riggi would boost the family's profits through shakedowns that targeted both local contractors and municipalities.

Like Sam the Plumber's repair and maintenance front, which allowed him to hide his illicit dealings behind the facade of a legal business entity, Riggi set out to hide his doings by establishing relationships and connections that would legitimize his profile and, hopefully, keep the attention of law enforcement away. These techniques, including payoffs to local politicians, supporting charities, and sponsoring development projects for youth sports leagues, allowed the DeCavalcante family under Riggi's leadership to continue profiting off of their various schemes from fraud and extortion to other serious crimes.

While Riggi's methods increased the flow of money into the organization, the blatant streams of payoffs and schemes that leaked out into the surrounding network of affiliates, labor unions, politicians, and local organizations were starting to garner unwanted attention. In fact, many of Riggi's businesses and dealings reeked of the exact kind of corruption that the Feds love to sniff out.

In 1990, after 8 years at the helm of the DeCavalcante family, Riggi was taken down by the law, being convicted on a number of counts, including extortion and racketeering. Sentenced to 12 years in the slammer, the clear choice was to delegate someone to run things on the street while still controlling the business from behind bars.

Riggi would find out that this tactic had varying success, as it reintroduced some of the instability that had plagued earlier iterations of the DeCavalcante family. The guy who Riggi would select to run the family's street operations while he was incarcerated was an easy choice. He had already selected Gaetano "Corky" Vastola as the leader of the ruling panel, and Vastola would now assume the role of street boss while Riggi was in prison.

This plan didn't last long, though, as Vastola was arrested shortly after being delegated this role. This is how underboss John D'Amato came into the picture, taking the cavalier move of appointing himself as acting boss in Riggi's absence.

John D'Amato: The Original Gay Mobster

Aside from D'Amato's presumptuous power grab and suspicions that he may have stolen money from the family, there was something else about him that just rubbed his fellow DeCavalcante family members the wrong way. Only one year into his stint heading up the family, he was raising suspicion among his own ranks.

Was it the fact that, in some ways, he seemed to be more loyal to the Gambino family than to his own guys from Jersey? Was it the suspicion that he had a grudge against Gaetano "Corky" Vastola and intended to off him once he got out of jail? Or, was it that there were rumors flying around that he liked to visit Manhattan sex clubs with his girlfriend, Kelly, where he'd allegedly engage in partner swapping and sexual acts of all kinds with both women and men?

Now, the Mafia's not a very forgiving place for people of varying inclinations, as the ranks of LCN tend to be filled with a lot of socially conservative guys, who do all the things that you'd expect of your typical, run-of-the-mill Italian–American, Jersey-born-and-bred guy. Even though mobsters have been known to party, sampling drugs of all kinds, spending late nights at strip clubs, visiting prostitutes, and cavorting with their multiple *goomars*, the average wiseguy is a pretty traditional guy who values family and follows a restrictive, old-world machismo that doesn't have much flexibility on issues like sexuality and gender.

One could say that LCN is about as far away as you can get from LGBTQ+ friendly, and D'Amato found this out the hard way. While he may have wanted to get whacked off by a guy in a sex club, instead, he ended up getting whacked by four shots from a pistol by a fellow DeCavalcante member in the backseat of a car in Brooklyn.

Like Vito Spatafore—capo of the Aprile crew whose sexuality is discovered by Meadow Soprano's boyfriend, Finn, when he rolls up early to a job site, only to witness a sex romp between Vito and a security guard—D'Amato must have had his own struggles in reconciling his identities as a bisexual man and a mobster. That said, Vito isn't the only *Sopranos* character with a more open approach to exploring his sexuality. One needs only to look at his ultimately ill-fated relationship with Janice Soprano to know that Ralph "Ralphie" Cifaretto is a masochistic fetishist, who's into edging, femdom, and gunplay.

But, back to Vito: In the *Sopranos* episode when he's spotted dancing at a gay nightclub by two associates out on a collection run, his decision to flee is not without justification. He knew that sticking around would have put him at risk of the same fate that D'Amato met in real life.

Deciding to go into hiding, Vito makes a smart move in letting the rumors around him cool off while D'Amato's error was to keep such a high profile. This manifested both in his bold power grab and the suspicious management style that suggested he wasn't trustworthy to his underlings. However different in their approach, both men, both in fiction and in real life, would come to meet similar fates at the hands of their own respective crews.

When Vito returns to Jersey after a stint in New Hampshire and runs into Tony at the mall, his proposal to come back into the organization is met with some reluctance. Tony knows that bringing a gay mobster back into the fold would cause some unwanted tensions between the DiMeo family and the family of extreme homophobe Phil Leotardo. After some consideration, it's clear that Vito has to go, and Tony orders the hit on him to avoid sparking conflict.

In the real-life happenings that left D'Amato riddled with bullets in January 1992, Anthony Capo, the DeCavalcante hitman who carried out the killing, testified: "Nobody's gonna respect us if we have a gay homosexual boss sitting down discussing La Cosa Nostra business" (Lehmann, 2003c, para. 3).

Picking up D'Amato from his girlfriend Kelly's house in Brooklyn, Anthony Capo and DeCavalcante associate Victor DiChiara, whose car they were driving that day, were invited to lunch by D'Amato. What the gay mobster got instead was a serving of lead, as the back seat filled up with his own blood, making such a messy scene that Capo decided DiChiara's car would have to be destroyed.

It's been suggested that one motive behind the hit on D'Amato was that another DeCavalcante capo, Anthony Rotondo, was also involved with D'Amato's girlfriend, Kelly. Rumor said that D'Amato and Kelly were in a fight before she suddenly decided to tell Rotondo about this revelation that D'Amato had participated in the alleged homosexual acts.

So, it's not known whether this conflict all came down to a lover's quarrel amid this odd triangular relationship or whether the truth behind the allegations was what led to the boss being offed. What is known is that once Rotondo informed ruling panel members Jake Amari and Stefano Vitabile of the allegations, they quickly sanctioned the hit, even though targeting an acting boss without discussing it first with the Commission is highly verboten. This set the path for Amari to come in as the next acting boss.

Jake Amari: The Real-Life Jackie Aprile

Gioacchino "Jake" Amari was a captain and well-respected member of Riggi's ruling panel even before he was promoted to acting boss. Known as a powerful labor racketeer in Newark during the 1980s, he almost went down with Riggi when they got caught committing extortion and running pension funds schemes in the early 1990s. Amari had an amicable relationship with Vitabile, who was one of the most powerful figures in the DeCavalcante crime family since Riggi installed him at the helm of the ruling panel when it was first created. Aside from his role on the panel together with Vitabile, Amari was fully in charge of all labor and construction racketeering operations for the DeCavalcante family.

Once Riggi was in the slammer and D'Amato came into the picture with his bold power grab, Amari stood together with Vitabile—solidifying their alliance as the two most powerful members of the group and a counterweight to D'Amato's actions. Once Anthony Rotondo heard from D'Amato's girlfriend about the couple's adventurous sex escapades, Amari and Vitabile were the first ones he went to with the gossip.

Ultimately, it was Amari and Vitabile who ordered the unsanctioned hit on D'Amato and were thereby obligated to inform the incarcerated Riggi of this news. Continuing as the two main power brokers of the family after taking out D'Amato, they attended a sit-down with representatives from the Gambino and Colombo families. The meeting wasn't in relation to D'Amato's unsanctioned offing but, rather, was called over a conflict surrounding a Little Italy social club that the DeCavalcante family had opened up in an attempt to recruit new guys and dig further into New York City territory.

The ruling panel members eventually came to an agreement with the Gambino and Colombo families, deciding that, going forward, the DeCavalcante family would have to restrict their pool of candidates and would only be able to make guys who lived within the bounds of New Jersey and South Philadelphia. From this point onward, they would not be able to recruit guys directly from New

York City but would continue to be permitted to operate their business interests there.

Amari was diagnosed with stomach cancer in the mid-1990s and was forced to cede more of his power to other members of the ruling panel as he died a slow, painful death. Some have made connections between this real-life mobster and Jackie Aprile Sr., the *Sopranos* character who passes away from the same terrible ailment that claimed Amari's life in 1997.

Even the guy who broke the news on D'Amato's sexual preference weighed in on the similarity. Once he turned rat, records of his courtroom testimony from 2003 suggest that not only was Anthony Rotondo aware of the TV show but that he himself recognized the parallels between this pair of real-life and fictional characters, noting that "every show you watch, more and more you pick somebody" (Scarpo, 2016, para.).

Upon Amari's passing, Riggi decided that the ruling panel would continue delegating major decisions and street action for the family, so three captains were promoted up to the panel: Vincent "Vinny Ocean" Palermo, Girolamo "Jimmy" Palermo, and Charles "Big Ears" Majuri. A lifelong DeCavalcante guy, Majuri was the son of former Elizabeth crew underboss and longtime DeCavalcante consigliere, Frank Majuri.

Some have said that Charles Majuri was furious at Riggi's decision, not so much at Riggi himself but at the two Palermos (who shared the same last name but were not related), that forced him to share power within the ruling panel.

CHAPTER 3
MAINTAINING THE FAMILY'S REPUTATION

While Riggi would remain incarcerated for the next 15 years, until 2012, the ruling panel continued to manage the important decisions that had to be made in his absence. The power vacuum that was left after Amari's passing led to a constant shuffling of roles and, most critically, a lack of the clear-cut management style that leaders like DeCavalcante and Riggi had instituted, which up to that point, had been largely successful in cultivating and maintaining a period of prolonged stability.

Those days were long gone, and the period of the mid to late 1990s saw the DeCavalcante family in slight disarray, as a series of bungled escapades of members and associates would come to attract the attention of law enforcement. At the cusp of the new millennium, the low profile from which the clan previously had benefited was put into the spotlight when a new TV series made its debut in 1999.

It was called *The Sopranos*, and while creator David Chase maintained that the inspiration for the series came from all different sources—including his childhood growing up in New Jersey, where Genovese family mobster Richie "The Boot" Boiardo was a neighbor of Chase's mother—the connections to the DeCavalcante family are clear.

The Inferiority Complex

When fictional mobster Carmine Lupertazzi uttered, "They're not a family, they're a glorified crew," one has to wonder whether David Chase and the *Sopranos* writing team had fashioned the fictional DiMeo family from some knowledge of the role that the DeCavalcante family had traditionally occupied within the greater New York City mob world, always operating among the shadows of the larger, more powerful Five Families.

Due to this dynamic, feelings of inferiority were something that had long existed within the DeCavalcante family, stretching all the way back to the early days of the Elizabeth and Newark families. Not only were they constantly referred to as "farmers" by the members of the Five Families, but they were also subject to the decisions of and the power dynamics within the Commission.

During Sam the Plumber's time, the family finally started to make some headway in tackling these issues and their slightly diminished profile within the criminal underworld. DeCavalcante was holding out for the possibility of winning a seat at the negotiating table of the Commission, wanting his family to not just have recognition as an independent entity but also to become the Sixth Family.

Transcripts of the bugged recordings from DeCavalcante's office at the Heating and Air Conditioning company include Sam lamenting the position he was always being put in by the Commission, expressing his displeasure over Joe Colombo having been appointed to the governing body at the suggestion of Carlo Gambino (Daly, 2017).

The inclusion of Colombo in the Commission put the hope that his namesake family might be considered for Commission membership to an end, as the Colombo organization descended directly from Joe Profaci's family—which had its own history of conflict with the proto-DeCavalcante organization, stemming from Profaci's clashes with Newark boss Gaspare D'Amico back in the bootlegging days.

The Media Blitz

Aside from the feelings of inferiority that still plagued the organization and contributed to the state of slight disarray in which they found themselves after Amari's passing, as well as the problems stemming from the shared-power mandate between Majuri and the Palermos, other issues began to emerge that would compromise the group's leadership and integrity as the clock ticked toward the end of the century.

Even before scrutiny was raised by the new mob-focused TV drama that premiered in 1999, ruling panel member Vincent "Vinny Ocean" Palermo had already been making waves, both in the press and the community in which he operated one of his businesses. This brewing culmination of forces would lead to further unwanted attention to his doings and bring further awareness of his status as a Mafia family member to the attention of the law.

Imagine if *Sopranos* character Silvio Dante had put his Bada Bing strip club in a different location, like the quiet residential neighborhood where Satriale's Pork Store is located, instead of out on Route 17. By putting his lucrative, mirror-clad smut palace in a neighborhood rather than a busy truck route out in Lodi, he would have been garnering unwanted attention from citizens and law enforcement alike. Well, that was exactly what Vinny Ocean did with his Rego Park, Queens-based strip club Wiggles.

Managing to gain heavy attention from both neighborhood activists as well as enforcers of New York City's strict cabaret and strip club laws, Wiggles as a business entity was obscured in a tangled web of ownership that was designed to keep Palermo officially outside the management structure and ownership of the club. That said, everyone knew it was his place, and he relished committing violation after violation while laughing in the face of concerned citizens who didn't want a nudie bar right on Queens Boulevard, in their family-oriented neighborhood.

Rudy Giuliani's coming in as mayor on January 1, 1994, helped reinforce and empower these NIMBY voices of concerned citizens who didn't want strip clubs in their neighborhoods. The new policies being drafted by city hall started to clean up formerly seedy areas, like Times Square, in an urban sweep campaign designed to snuff all kinds of vice, but namely sex and drugs, off the streets of the Big Apple.

By the time Palermo opened up Wiggles on Queens Boulevard in July 1994, the vice squad of concerned citizens, feeling empowered by the government-driven cleanup efforts already in full force, were fully mobilized. Wiggles was picketed by concerned citizens almost every night once it opened, even making it a constitutional issue by proclaiming that the club was just exercising its First Amendment rights.

Palermo's response to this challenge was not to remain low-key about drowning out these voices; instead, he brashly chose to combat the protesters. He placed signs at the entrance encouraging patrons to exercise their constitutional rights by coming in to enjoy a promotional deal, which included free admission, a complimentary buffet, and the promise to gaze at topless girls, all for the cost of zero dollars! But Vinny Ocean didn't stop there. He took things even further, all the way to the point of filing a civil free-speech lawsuit against the protesters.

On September 1, 1994, Palermo's lawyer, Stanley Meyer, filed a lawsuit in the New York Supreme Court, alleging that the protesters outside Wiggles were violating the business's right of "freedom of expression." Requesting that the judge rule an immediate halt to the protests, Meyer cited the fact that protesters' intrusions included violating customers' privacy rights by photographing them coming in and out of the club, as well as by taking pictures of their license plates (Smith, 2003).

Like the *Sopranos* episode when Tony's crew, armed with clubs and Italian–American pride rush to a Columbus Day protest being held by Native American anticolonial activists, Palermo's free-speech episode highlights what happens when politics and mob interests collide.

While some have written off Season 4, Episode 3 as one of the worst episodes of the entire series, it does a great job of showing how stubborn and principled mobsters can be, however problematic their politics and views. Targets of revenge and the grudges held between members are often contained within the inner networks and ties of mobsters. But, the real-life case of Vinny Ocean's Wiggles strip club and the *Sopranos* episode both show what happens during the rare moments when the focus of mob interest crystallizes around a political or social issue and leaks out from the closed cell of the criminal underworld, onto the general public

While in the *Sopranos* episode it was an issue of Italian–American pride, and in the real-life Wiggles saga it was an issue of business-turned-political-vendetta, both stories demonstrate that all publicity is good publicity, except in the case of the mob. These kinds of actions put participating members at risk of being exposed and drawing further attention to their dealings, even when their illegal activities were carried out behind a legitimate front, such as Wiggles or Silvio's fictional Bada Bing.

The Bungled Heist

Vinny Ocean Palermo's brash disregard for the tried-and-true practice of not making a spectacle out of yourself as a made guy reflected the slight disarray in which the modern incarnation of the DeCavalcante family found itself. It was a familiar place for the family to be in; after all, it had become a defining characteristic of the family, only interrupted sporadically by brief periods of stability throughout its history.

It wasn't Vinny Ocean's antics but yet another incident around this time that would make the family the laughingstock of their mob circles as well as the tabloid news media. And this one was carried out not by a capo but by a low-level DeCavalcante associate. Before the twin towers of the World Trade Center were brought down by terrorists, but after they had already been targeted in a 1993 car bombing, there was a bank heist that took place within the iconic Financial District skyscrapers, making news headlines that left the general public and wiseguys alike scratching their heads.

Toward the end of 1997, Ralph "Ralphie" Guarino, a DeCavalcante associate, hatched a plan to snag bags of cash from a Bank of America branch office that was housed in the World Trade Center. The thieves he contracted the job out to were able to make off with around $1 million, but the bone-headed bandits didn't even notice that the majority of the cash they grabbed was in foreign currencies, making it extremely difficult to launder in any organized and logical fashion.

The greenbacks left on the table at the crime scene totaled $1.6 million, the majority of which was sitting right at the bottom of the money bags that the crooks sliced open and plundered. Aside from these unfortunate realities—not only that a ton of cash was left on the table but also that Guarino was now stuck with difficult-to-deal-with stacks of foreign banknotes—the bandits also managed to get captured in the act by over 55 security cameras. The following day, they were all over the TV and printed in all of the newspapers.

Only one of the guys, the leader of the group of thugs that Guarino contracted the job out to, a guy named Richie Gillette, was smart enough to pull a hood over his face before the men pulled ski masks over their faces. The other two guys were all over the media, making this bungled caper into a full-on comic media spectacle. The guys were easily tracked down, and Guarino was forced to fork over

$20,000 to each of them, leaving him with piles and piles of yen and liras to himself (Smith, 2003).

This bungled crime that the media spun into a full-blown spectacle was characteristic of the time period, putting DeCavalcante members and associates in the spotlight and drawing attention that likely rubbed many in the low-profile New Jersey clan the wrong way.

The Consequences of Discord

The period of the mid to late 1990s represented a transitional phase for the DeCavalcante family. With Riggi locked up and with ruling panel members like Vinny Ocean Palermo, and even low-level guys like Ralphie Guarino, making a mockery of the organization through their misguided and bungled capers, which attracted greater attention to their business interests and illegal doings, things started to fall apart. The Feds were closing in, and the period between 1999 and 2005 would see a mass roundup of DeCavalcante family members and associates.

Almost threatening to put an end to the family as it was known, the mass arrests included seven capos within the family. This would severely compromise the already fragile power structure that had been in place since Amari passed away, when Riggi brought Majuri, Vinny Ocean Palermo, and Jimmy Palermo into the ruling panel.

While the mechanisms that precipitated the organization's downfall were already put into motion, another phenomenon began to come into the picture, and it was one that would rapidly accelerate the dismantling of the family's hierarchy and its ability to stay afloat.

A rat infestation was imminent. While the details of the deals cut by these two-faced individuals who ratted out members of their own family will be focused on in more depth in a later chapter of this book, it's important to note that the challenges faced by the DeCavalcante family in this era were multilateral and threatened to swallow them up whole.

Riggi's Extended Sentence

When sentenced back in 1992, Riggi's initial release date was set to be 2003. The reason he ended up serving an extended sentence was that, in the web of chaos spun by the wave of ratting-out that plagued the DeCavalcante family, Riggi got implicated in some of his past dealings. Once uncovered by informants, these buried secrets made their way into the hands of prosecutors.

Due to the wave of informants that racked the organization, it came to be that, while already serving his initial prison term, Riggi faced additional charges for being implicated in the 1989 murder of Fred Weiss, a Staten Island property developer who had a hit ordered on him by none other than John Gotti himself. Gotti feared that Weiss, a former Staten Island Advance journalist, would go to the police with his knowledge of an illegal medical-waste dumping scheme, and so, he had the DeCavalcante family under Riggi's command "take care" of the matter.

Serving an extended sentence until 2012, Riggi was released from the Federal Medical Center in Devens, Massachusetts on November

27, 2012, at the age of 87. While some viewed the extended sentence he received in 2003 as, essentially, a life sentence, Riggi managed to hang on until 90, living the last 3 years of his life as a free man and finally passing away on August 3, 2015.

The Old Man

In the wave of charges that came from 2000 until 2003 and extended Riggi's prison term, a whole bunch of other guys were also brought down, including acting underboss and ruling panel member Girolamo "Jimmy" Palermo. With Riggi's ruling panel now compromised by the wave of rats and indictments, somebody had to step in and take control.

Assuming the de facto leadership role, as at the time he was the oldest member of the family, Joseph Miranda, whose nickname was "The Old Man," stepped in to try and steady the creaky vessel that the DeCavalcante family had become. This old-timer got made under Sam the Plumber, so he'd been around for a long time and was likely dismayed by the state he saw the family in at the time he took command.

Operating out of a bar in Elizabeth, this old-school Mafia boss began an initiative to recruit some new guys, but as his nickname suggested, the old-timer didn't have any of the fresh ideas that were needed to carry the family into the 21st century.

Miranda's attempts at repairing the family by bringing in a few new members were not effective in affronting the huge challenges of continued operations during this time. After three years at the helm, The Old Man decided to pass his role down to a younger guy, a Sicilian from Ribera named Francesco Guarraci, toward the end of 2006.

Guarraci Steps In

Guarraci got made under John Riggi in the late 1980s and served as a living link to the group's roots in Ribera, Sicily. He was a frequent presence at the family's Ribera Club at 408 Palmer Street in Elizabeth, where he was said to be a kind of manager, although his official "job" was as a foreman in the historically DeCavalcante family-run labor union Local 394.

This local labor union had been a main source of income for the DeCavalcante family since the 1930s. Through their control of the union over many decades, the family made substantial sums of money annually by extorting contractors and engaging in other corrupt labor practices.

Having arrived stateside in 1967, Guarraci made his way up the ranks until he was named acting boss in 2006, with Miranda stepping down to underboss. At this time, both Guarraci and Miranda still reported to Riggi from his prison cell and were responsible for carrying out any of his orders. Living in a modest house in Elizabeth, Guarraci tried to keep a low profile and was not named in any of the indictments that the family was contending with at the time.

Known as a boss who was tough but also well liked, some thought that Francesco Guarraci had prospects to become the next great leader of the family, perhaps that he would even be able to pull things together, to unify and maybe even tighten up the business dealings of the family, which would lead to greater sources of revenue the likes of what Sam The Plumber was able to bring in during his time.

Aside from his Ribera, Sicily, heritage, Guarraci was seen by some as the perfect guy to step up, as he was largely unknown to law enforcement and even to many within the group itself. Somebody like Guarraci taking over would finally mark a shift in the spectacle that had been swirling around the small New Jersey outfit since the leadership of bosses like Vinny Ocean Palermo and low-level guys like Ralphie Guarino, who through their audacious and public-facing escapades ended up compromising the integrity and continued well-being of the organization.

That said, despite his low-key, mild-mannered approach to business within the family, Guarraci had a violent side to his personality that would peep out from time to time. Like the *Sopranos* episode in which Richie Aprile pays a visit to Beansie, the proprietor of a local pizzeria that he's trying to extort, Guarraci got in trouble for a similar incident he pulled at a Washington Township pizzeria in 2009.

Guarraci, along with Michael "Mikey Red" Nobile, John Koster, and two other unnamed individuals, entered Lenny's Pizza on a summer's evening and tried to shake down the place. The manager of the restaurant, whose owner had recently passed away, was not receptive to the demands of the goombahs who suddenly appeared in his shop. Informing the manager and restaurant workers that, in the absence of the old owner, Guarraci was now in charge of the place, Guarraci's guys demanded that the manager hand over the money and receipts.

When the manager refused to comply with the demands, the guys threatened him and began screaming at him and physically restraining the manager to prevent him from making a phone call. While the incident didn't end with the kind of violent beating that Richie Aprile dealt out to Beansie in *The Sopranos*, it did come close to boiling over.

A customer that witnessed the attempted shakedown was able to call 911, relaying to the operator that the scene over there was like something out of *The Sopranos*. The police rolled up, and all of the individuals involved in the scuff-up were questioned. The guys who accompanied Guarraci that day were arrested in February of the following year on charges related to this incident and their attempted extortion of the pizzeria.

While Guarraci made news headlines and had the police at his doorstep following the pizzeria escapade, it wouldn't be long until another DeCavalcante captain would start attracting more attention from law enforcement. Though, this time, it wouldn't be for local shakedowns and threats but for some long-distance dealings in New Jersey organized crime. The guy's name was Charles "Beeps" Stango.

Trouble in Las Vegas

Around the same time that John Riggi was getting out of prison in 2012, another DeCavalcante guy was released. He was a longtime DeCavalcante *caporegime* named Charles "Beeps" Stango, and he was getting out of prison just in time to pick up some of the slack in various crises that the early and mid-2000s had brought to the family. Once he was free, he was now able to become a reliable earner again. Though Stango was an Elizabeth guy, upon release from prison, he moved to Henderson, Nevada, a Las Vegas suburb.

While the stereotypes about wiseguys and their love of Sin City rings true, Stango wasn't just out in the desert of the American Southwest to hit the craps table; rather, he'd be running his crew of DeCavalcante soldiers and associates remotely, giving him some physical distance from the places where many of his orders were being carried out.

Though Stango did have some local schemes going out in Vegas, and had established some connections and revenue sources in New Orleans and Los Angeles as well, his main gig was running his crew's operations in Toms River, a Jersey Shore township that's an hour south of the family's base in Elizabeth. Making business deals on drugs and prostitution—and even ordering hits on guys over the phone—Stango's Vegas outpost may have allowed him to enjoy the desert sun, but it didn't prevent him from getting tied up in the same kind of law enforcement scrutiny and legal trouble that had already been plaguing the DeCavalcante family for over a decade.

Soon enough, Stango would get tied up in a number of difficult issues, as an undercover agent had infiltrated his crew. Aside from the issues caused by Stango's illicit business interests and plots being uncovered by the FBI, there was another force creeping in, though a familiar one: the Gambinos.

Though under Riggi's command, the DeCavalcante family's relationship with the Five Families had been strong. Riggi was seen as a strong, independent leader by insiders and other mob leaders alike. While he did order hits on behalf of other guys, as apparent in the 1989 Fred Weiss murder, Riggi always maintained and projected autonomy. From the time of D'Amato's ill-fated tenure as boss, there had been rising insider concerns about the encroachment of a certain "Dapper Don" on DeCavalcante affairs. From the late 1980s onward, John Gotti and the Gambino family would continue to be influential in DeCavalcante family doings and decision-making, even after Gotti passed away in 2002.

Charles Stango lamented the fact that the New Jersey family of which he was a boss now flew under the flag of the larger New York outfit, peppering his conversations with self-deprecating phrases, such as "now we run under the fuckin' Gambinos" (Amoruso, 2015, para. 3).

Adding to the feelings of inferiority that were already present within the DeCavalcante family, this Jersey crew of "farmers" had many challenges to contend with during their more contemporary incarnation. Stango continued as boss of his crew until 2015, when charges were brought against him as well as his son, Anthony Stango, DeCavalcante family consigliere Frank "Shipe" Nigro, and associate Paul "Knuckles" Colella on charges of narcotics, prostitution, and conspiracy to commit murder.

In total, 10 DeCavalcante members and associates were arrested in March 2015, and then, with John Riggi's passing a few months later, the family was now depending fully on acting boss Francesco Guarraci for guidance and leadership.

Though Guarraci was not named in any of the indictments that stemmed from the infiltration of Stango's crew, ensuring that the highest levels of the family leadership chain would remain unscathed, the charges and indictments began to pile up, putting a considerable amount of stress on the organization and their operations.

Charged with various narcotics, prostitution, and contraband-cigarette violations, Charles Stango's son, Anthony, with whom he was planning to open a high-end call service in Toms River, was sent off to prison in 2016 while his dad was still on trial. And the following year, Charles Stango himself would be put away to serve a 10-year sentence.

With other DeCavalcante members and associates who were implicated in the findings of the undercover investigation also getting locked up on drug charges at this time, the family was also met by the unfortunately timed passing of acting boss Francesco Guarraci in April 2016.

Charles "Big Ears" Majuri

Assuming de facto control of the organization upon Guarraci's death, longtime DeCavalcante high-ranking member Frank "Big Ears" Majuri had finally made it to the top. A trusted ruling panel member and a constant presence in the organization, upon finally inheriting sovereign leadership of the group, Majuri must have found himself in an unfamiliar position and experienced a wide range of feelings about his arrival as top guy. While he had been upset at Riggi's appointing Vinny Ocean and Jimmy Palermo to the ruling panel back in the 1990s, and for having been forced to share power beside them for so long, he now found himself not only stuck with the legacy of a weary and downtrodden family that had seen better times but also under the constant scrutiny of law enforcement efforts to end them for good.

Aside from the fact that Majuri was the oldest surviving member of the family and that many of the guys that he previously depended on were either imprisoned, dead, rats, or worse, he also had to meet the demands of a changing reality and navigate what it meant to be a Mafia boss in the 21st century.

Majuri was and is an old-school mob guy, tracing his roots in the family back to his father, Frank Majuri, who was an Elizabeth underboss under Nick Delmore. Although he was caught up, like many members were, in the series of busts that shook the group in the late 1990s, he was heavily implicated in the courtroom testimony of rats, and in 2000, he was indicted on 19 counts, having been charged with various illicit gambling offenses, racketeering, extortion, and conspiracy to commit murder.

Though Majuri remained a free man as the trials progressed, based on his indictments for bookmaking and illegal gambling, he was banned from entering any casino in the state of New Jersey and was forced to remain on the sidelines of the organization to avoid further charges and violations while court cases were still pending. He was forced to just watch as The Old Man, Joseph "Joe" Miranda, struggled to keep things afloat. In 2006, Majuri was finally convicted of his crimes and sent off to prison, where he would remain until 2009.

Upon his release from prison, Majuri encountered a changed organization: With Riggi still locked up and the Sicilian Guarraci in charge, the ruling panel had long been dismantled, and the power structure had changed once again, with Miranda having stepped down to underboss when Majuri was sent off to prison. Majuri had survived a lot so far, including multiple attempts on his own life, the most notable ones stemming from his own inner circle.

Back when Riggi first appointed the guys to head up the ruling panel, Vinny Ocean and Jimmy Palermo knew that Majuri had attempted to put a hit out on them. Majuri's plan was foiled when the guy he contracted it out to, Jimmy Gallo, let the guys know they were being targeted rather than carry out the deed.

The response devised by Vinny Ocean and Jimmy Palermo was to give it right back—contracting the same guy, Jimmy Gallo, along with Anthony Capo, the hitman that whacked John D'Amato, to put Majuri in his grave. This assassination attempt was foiled when Gallo, Capo, and DeCavalcante associate Joseph "Joey O" Masella pulled up to do the deed and, as they were waiting for Majuri to come out of his house, noticed that there was a state trooper's police car parked right next door.

Seeing himself as a survivor in many ways, and with his inner-group rivalries no longer at the forefront, Majuri finally had the mandate to lead. But the feelings of betrayal and mistrust must have remained, especially the stinging fact that Vinny Ocean and Anthony Capo's ratting on him was what ultimately led to his imprisonment. Jimmy Palermo, who also crossed Majuri in the planned hit attempt against him, had already died back in 2014, so there was no real point in holding a grudge against him anymore. Moreover, Majuri had enough of his own issues on the table, and it was time for him to get to business cementing the legacy of the sometimes-denigrated but all-around respected family that boasts a unique born-and-bred New Jersey heritage, the family they call DeCavalcante.

Majuri stands as the boss of the family up until the present day, maintaining strong connections that go all the way back to his father, Frank, whose own history with the family went all the way back to the bootlegging days. Whether or not Majuri is able to keep the DeCavalcantes relevant while addressing the concerns of their current dealings is yet to be known.

While much information on the current state of the family and the full reach of their business doings is under tight wraps for obvious reasons, details of current business dealings and scandals of the group are overviewed in Chapter 7, in which they're examined in as much detail as possible without violating any existing privacy laws and, crucially, without getting a hit put out on our heads over here at Mafia Library.

CHAPTER 4
JERSEY BOYS

What makes a Jersey Boy? As you'll find out in this book, it's not all about *gabagool* and wearing tracksuits as some stereotypical portrayals of Italian–American life might have you believe. In fact, Italian–American history in New York and New Jersey has a rich cultural history, not all of which is organized crime adjacent. The majority of immigrants who took the risk and hopped a ship over to Ellis Island were only seeking out a better existence and looking to secure a prosperous future for their families in the land of opportunity.

Italian–American Communities in New Jersey

The First Wave of Immigration

Italians began immigrating to New York City in large numbers during the late 19th century, driven by a variety of factors, including economic hardship and political instability in their home country. Many of the immigrants who came over were from Southern Italy and were drawn to America by the promise of greater economic opportunities and a better standard of living.

One of the primary reasons for Italian immigration to New York City was the economic realities in Italy at the time. The 1861 unification of the country took the disparate former kingdoms that made up the Italian Peninsula and brought them together under the Kingdom of Italy. For the first time in its history, citizens from Calabria all the way to the Italian Alps were subject to the same laws and policies, an impressive territorial and cultural reach that put the poorer Southern Italians at an economic disadvantage compared to the heavily industrialized North.

Much of the South was still primarily an agricultural society, and many rural areas were characterized by poverty and a lack of education. As the economic engines of the North were experiencing a period of rapid industrialization, migrants from the South were drawn to these urban centers, causing a decline in the traditional agricultural work that took place in their home regions. This contributed further to the economic decline in the southern regions of Italy, as the capable, young men were lured elsewhere, and manpower, resources, and economic activity dried up.

While some migrants found opportunities in the richer, more industrialized Northern Italy, others were interested in immigrating to the United States, which was experiencing a period of tremendous economic growth and expansion during this time. The labor market in the United States was far greater even than that of industrialized North Italy, and young, adventurous men were ready to make their passage to this land of opportunity.

New York City was the main immigration port for Europeans crossing the Atlantic, and it so happened that it was also a major hub of burgeoning industry and commerce. Many Italians decided to stay in the city once they passed the gates of Ellis Island, seeing it as a place where opportunity abounded and where they might encounter well-paying jobs and the better standard of living they were after.

When Italians first arrived in New York City, they often took on low-paying jobs in the city's industrial sectors, such as garment manufacturing and construction. Many worked as unskilled laborers, as factory workers, dockworkers, and domestic helpers. However, as Italian communities became more established in the city, many of the immigrants started to open their own businesses and become entrepreneurs, creating their own enclaves where they settled.

Recently arrived Italians settled in various neighborhoods throughout the city, but they were particularly concentrated in certain areas, such as the Lower East Side and East Harlem. These neighborhoods were often characterized by overcrowded tenement buildings with poor living conditions, but they were also home to a vibrant and tight-knit Italian–American community. Many of these neighborhoods also had a strong sense of community and cultural identity, with many Italian-owned businesses, churches, and social clubs.

As the 20th century progressed, first-generation Italian immigrants and their families began to move out of these neighborhoods and into other parts of the city, to the outer boroughs of New York City, and to New Jersey.

Elizabeth and Newark

The neighboring cities of Elizabeth and Newark divide Union and Essex Counties along the shared water border of Newark Bay.

According to historical data, these areas were already beginning to house significant Italian immigrant populations in the late 19th century. An 1890 survey map shows that there were over 1,000 Italians living in Essex County and 500–1,000 living in Union County (New Jersey Italian and Italian American Commission, 2010).

Overall, the New Jersey of this time would be almost unrecognizable today, still featuring sprawling agricultural lands and vast open spaces. But, while this was true of the state overall, the cities of Newark and Elizabeth were already dense urban centers that were heavily industrialized, even by the mid-1800s when the first Italian immigrants began arriving in America. In fact, these port cities were important centers of commerce dating all the way back to the 1660s, and they had well-established histories as industrial centers for both manufacturing and shipping.

The influx of Italian immigrants to Essex and Union Counties began in the late 19th century and continued through the early 20th century, with the majority arriving between 1890 and 1920. Newark and Elizabeth, with their proximity to New York City and their burgeoning industrial economies, proved to be attractive destinations for recently arrived immigrants. In Newark, the growing manufacturing and construction industries provided jobs for Italian immigrants while, in Elizabeth, many found work in the city's port and on the nearby railroad lines.

As the number of Italian immigrants in Newark and Elizabeth grew, so did the number of Italian–American businesses and organizations in these cities. Italian grocery stores, cafes, and bakeries were a common sight, and many immigrants also opened their own businesses, such as barber shops and tailoring shops. Italian-American social clubs, like the Ribera Club in Elizabeth, were also established, providing a sense of community and support for the immigrants. The Italian immigrants who settled in New Jersey's industrial core faced many challenges as they adjusted to life in a new country.

Language barriers, discrimination, and poverty were common problems that they faced. Despite these difficulties, many Italian immigrants were able to build successful lives in Newark and Elizabeth, and their contributions to these cities were significant. The Italian immigrants who settled there also made lasting contributions to the cities' political and cultural landscapes. Many Italian-American politicians and civic leaders emerged from these communities, as would many a wiseguy.

In Newark, one of the areas that Italian immigrants flocked to was the North Ward, where many settled and established businesses. The North Ward was also home to the largest Italian-American festival in the state, the Feast of Mount Carmel, which celebrated the patron saint of the North Ward's Italian-American community. The event was held annually and attracted thousands of visitors from all over the state.

In Elizabeth, the Peterstown neighborhood was the heart of the Italian-American community. The neighborhood was home to many Italian-American businesses, such as bakeries, butcher shops, and restaurants. The neighborhood was also home to the St.

Anthony of Padua Church, the largest Italian–American church in Elizabeth.

In 1930, the inaugural festival in honor of St. Rocco began in the Peterstown neighborhood, and it would continue to be an always-anticipated and well-attended affair for many years. The St. Rocco Feast was first envisioned by Vincenzo Gogliardo, an Italian immigrant who brought the tradition of honoring St. Rocco from his hometown of Savoia di Lucania in the Potenza province of Italy to Elizabeth.

The event, which was held over the weekend after August 16, the exact date of the Feast Day of St. Rocco, grew from a small event held in front of Gogliardo's home to a 3-day celebration that moved to Spencer Street. For years, it was the largest festival in Union County, though sadly it ended in 1988.

The Ribera Club and Other Hangouts

Although the beloved St. Rocco festival ended in 1988, the presence of Italian social clubs and other organizations continued in the area, some to this day. The Ribera Club is one of them. It was the place that DeCavalcante family boss Francesco "Frank" Guarraci ran from 1989 up until his death in 2016. The original location of the clubhouse was at 620 3rd Avenue at the corner of John Street in Elizabeth.

The building that houses the Ribera Club today was constructed on the lot of 412–416 Palmer Street (though according to Google Maps, the address of the building today is 406), and it dates back to 2008. But, the history of the club goes way back before Guarraci's time, even back to the time before the proto-DeCavalcante family was born when Stefano Badami took over the combined Elizabeth–Newark families after Newark boss Gaspare D'Amico fled for his life.

The club was founded in 1923 by immigrants who came to Elizabeth from the town of Ribera, Sicily. When Ribera native Francesco "Frank" Guarraci took it over in 1989, it must have represented a full circle for many members of the group. With a younger Sicilian immigrant taking over the club's operations, it connected the current day with the group's past and shared cultural heritage.

These blood connections likely helped solidify Guarraci's success as DeCavalcante family boss and also helped to further solidify his standing both within the club and the family. As mentioned before, Guarraci was well liked already and known to be a fair and even-keeled leader, just what the family needed with Riggi still locked up and stability within the clan in the same constant flux as it had been throughout almost its entire history.

When Guarraci was first becoming an important fixture at the Ribera Club in the late 1980s, it would have still been based at the old clubhouse location back at 620 3rd Avenue. By the time plans were in the works for the new structure at Palmer Street, Guarraci was well into his tenure as Ribera Club manager and would have just been starting his role as DeCavalcante family boss.

The fact that Guarraci assumed power in 2006 and this new clubhouse popped up just 2 years later suggests that it may have been a pet project of Guarraci's own and that, during his time managing the space at 3rd Avenue, he may have been thinking about moving the club to a better location for some time. Strategically placed at the end of a dead-end road, undercover agent "Giovanni Rocco" in his book *Giovanni's Ring* mentioned that there was only one door into and one door out of 406 Palmer Street (though this is unverified and, if it were true, likely would not conform to strict local fire codes).

The ribbon was cut for the grand opening of this new building on September 21, 2008, in celebration of the Ribera Club's 85-year anniversary. In the August–September 2008 issue of *Around About Peterstown*, a local rag published by Joe Renna and the Sons of Peterstown Sports Club, the new Ribera Club facility was described as "the organization's new clubhouse along with a game room, a cafe, and a meeting hall that can be used for social events" ("Ribera Club Celebrates," 2008, para. 2). The bimonthly newsletter also mentioned that the rear of the building features an outdoor patio space with a brick pizza oven.

The modest brick-face building with slightly audacious white-pillar columns was one of the modest but important achievements during Guarraci's stint as boss, and it's still recognized today as the unofficial headquarters of the DeCavalcante family. While the description of the building featured in *Around About Peterstown* made mention of the club's plan to make use of some of their 4,000-square-foot clubhouse as a classroom to teach Italian language and history classes, not much is known about what really goes on inside the space today.

The public-facing image of the Ribera Club is one of a cultural heritage organization, not as the clubhouse of a crime syndicate.

Sponsoring fundraising events to benefit scholarship programs, the club projects an image of being a responsible, socially invested organization, but those in the know, both inside and outside the community, know that the place is Mafia central as the DeCavalcante family's brick-and-mortar location.

As far as the various types of Mafia business that occur inside the building go, it's been suggested that it may serve as the center of recruiting operations for the family, especially when it comes to taking guys over directly from Sicily. So, if the Naples-born *Sopranos* character Furio Giunta was a real-life recruit in the DeCavalcante family, he likely would have passed through the columns of the Ribera Club as one of his first stops fresh off the plane.

In the interest of keeping law enforcement at bay, and probably in an authentic gesture of serving the community, the club does operate as a legitimate business, renting its space out as a function and event hall to private parties. Though the club was a known wiseguy hangout, and seems to play an important role in the Sicily–Elizabeth recruitment pipeline, it certainly isn't the only spot in town where DeCavalcante guys go to kick back and socialize with fellow members and associates.

According to Giovanni Rocco, the pseudonym of an undercover agent who infiltrated the DeCavalcante family, there was another local hangout that DeCavalcante guys frequented. This one looked a little more like Tony's hangout in the back of Satriale's Pork Store, with poker tables and horizontal blinds to block out any intrusive eyes.

In a self-referencing collision of meta forces, Rocco also reported that the walls of this more low-key DeCavalcante hangout were filled with *Sopranos* posters and other Mafia-related regalia (Rocco & Schofield, 2021)—again demonstrating that not only was the DeCavalcante family aware of the *Sopranos* connections that others pointed out and had already been discussed within the family but that some were also big-enough fans of the show to plaster the walls of their hangout spot with *Sopranos* memorabilia.

The Laws of the Streets

Sicilian immigrants who settled in the cities of Elizabeth and Newark in the late 19th and early 20th centuries established their own set of laws to govern their communities. These laws were often based on traditional Sicilian customs and values and were enforced by the community's leaders. They were designed to maintain order while protecting the interests of the community. Often through strict codes of honor and personal conduct, such as omertà, Sicilians governed themselves while protecting their communities from outside interference.

While the use of violence was not a core principle that guided these principled immigrants, they were not afraid to use it when necessary. This approach to self-governing, self-policing, and score-settling within the community was often seen as suspicious by outsiders, who were not familiar with the cultural norms and values of the Sicilian community.

The insular and family-centric culture of Sicilian immigrants contributed to their reputation for being suspicious or, sometimes, even superstitious to those outside the fold. Often forming tight-knit communities based on extended family ties, they were known to be fiercely loyal to their families and their community. This strong sense of loyalty and community often made them seem closed off and unapproachable to Americans, who'd already been in the country for a couple of generations, as well as to other immigrant communities, who may have perceived Sicilians as being particularly unwilling to integrate into American society. Their adherence to traditional customs and beliefs, such as the use of folk healing practices, may have also contributed to them being perceived as superstitious by outsiders.

The laws of the streets established by Sicilian–American immigrants at the time were different from what others were used to and were certainly contributing factors to the way they were perceived by outsiders. This led Sicilian communities to sometimes face the harsh realities of discrimination, even coming from other Italian-immigrant groups. While the vast majority of Italian immigrants that came to New York and New Jersey were from Southern Italy, they did not always exhibit solidarity toward each other, as they each came from varying and unique languages, cultures, and traditions.

Organized Crime in New Jersey

The history of organized crime in New Jersey goes back to the early days and the arrival of Italian–American immigrants in New York City. These immigrants brought with them a tradition of secret societies and criminal organizations, which would eventually evolve into the modern-day organized-crime groups that are known today.

One of the earliest known organized-crime groups in New York was the Black Hand, a secret society that operated in the early 1900s. The Black Hand was made up of Italian–American immigrants and targeted other immigrants, extorting money and committing other crimes. The group was known for its use of violence and intimidation tactics, and it was eventually broken up by law enforcement in the 1920s.

As the Elizabeth and Newark families battled things out in New Jersey, eventually culminating in D'Amico's ouster from Newark, across the river in downtown Manhattan, there was another early organized-crime group called the Five Points Gang that was active in the 1920s and 1930s. The gang was founded by Italian–American Paul Kelly (real name: Paolo Antonio Vaccarelli) and made up of immigrants from a few different nationalities, though the majority of them were Irish. They were involved in a variety of criminal activities, including extortion, racketeering, and murder. Many famous mobsters, including Al Capone, Lucky Luciano, and Meyer Lansky, got their start as members of this gang.

In the post-World War II era, the organized-crime scene in New Jersey began to shift toward more traditional organized-crime groups, such as the Mafia. It was only during this time that the DeCavalcante family began to be widely known throughout the area, even though their origins extended way back to the bootlegging days of the Elizabeth–Newark family under Stefano Badami.

By the time Sam the Plumber came into the picture, the DeCavalcante crime family was thought of as the most powerful and well-known organized-crime group in New Jersey. Known for their involvement in a wide range of criminal activities, including racketeering, extortion, and murder, they were feared throughout the state. During this era, the Five Families of the LCN were also operating heavily in New Jersey, particularly the Gambino family. Controlling many of the criminal activities in the state, the Gambinos held a tight grip on the construction industry and also had control over the unions, which helped them make money and launder their illegal gains.

The Gambino family would eventually make a business of grabbing power from other families operating in New Jersey under famous capo John Gotti. Gotti's coming into power in 1985 would lead to an encroachment on the DeCavalcante family's autonomy from the late 1980s onward and to power grabs of business and territory with other LCN crime families, such as the Genovese family.

In recent years, law enforcement has made significant strides in dismantling organized-crime groups in New Jersey. In the 1980s, the FBI's "Operation Ironclad" targeted the DeCavalcante crime family and other organized-crime groups in New Jersey, leading to the arrest and conviction of numerous high-ranking members. In the following years, the government continued its efforts to combat organized crime, including the use of the Racketeer Influenced and Corrupt Organizations (RICO) Act to target and prosecute organized-crime groups.

Overall, the history of organized crime in New Jersey is a complex and ongoing one. From the early days of the Black Hand and the Five Points Gang to the powerful organized-crime groups of the mid-20th century to the government's ongoing efforts to combat organized crime in recent years, the state has seen a wide range of criminal organizations and activities. While law enforcement has made significant strides in dismantling these groups, the reality is that organized crime continues to have a significant presence in the Garden State.

CHAPTER 5
FIVE FAMILIES CONNECTIONS

In the 2004 status report *The Changing Face of Organized Crime in New Jersey*, issued by the State of New Jersey's Commission of Investigation, there are references to the "Seven Families" of the New York–New Jersey–Philadelphia region. Including the DeCavalcante family, as well as the Bruno family (aka Bruno-Scarfo family, aka the Philadelphia crime family), the authors of the report were certainly exercising some creative license in naming these smaller outfits as if they shared equal standing among the Five Families, though they were not without reason for doing so.

The DeCavalcante family never managed to win a seat on LCN's Commission, the governing body that comprised members of the Gambino, Lucchese, Colombo, Bonanno, and Genovese families. However, their inclusion in the State of New Jersey's report as the "Sixth Family" recognizes not just their long history but also their continued presence in the region and their sustained contributions toward shaping the face of modern organized crime in the Garden State.

Sam the Plumber had always hoped that the Commission would fully accept the family he spent so much effort modernizing into their fold, and they did for the most part. But, by constantly withholding full membership, the Five Families always managed to keep the family of New Jersey "farmers" at arm's length. While these measures were likely taken not to encroach on the DeCavalcante's autonomy but rather in the interest of continued collaboration with the smaller Jersey-born-and-bred family, they did end up, at many times, both compromising the independence of the group as well as cultivating feelings of slight inadequacy within the ranks.

Flying Under the Flag of the Gambinos

By the early to mid-1990s, the Gambino family and its capo—Dapper Don himself, Mr. John Gotti—were household names. Referenced in TV shows and comedy routines, the New York underworld had found the spotlight in mainstream entertainment, setting things up for the pop-culture collision that would come later in the decade when the similarities between real-life criminals in the DeCavalcante family and characters on *The Sopranos* would become more apparent and start to blur the lines dividing TV and reality.

Gotti was a charismatic and ostentatious presence in New York as a standover from the glitzier, more gaudy 1980s. Like Donald Trump, who at the time still relished the New York tabloid press's blessings of free PR, John Gotti was another crook with panache who, for whatever reasons, connected with the public at the time and fueled their collective fantasies around the allure of business and crime.

While Trump's game was real estate and "deals," Gotti's game was also "deals," except his were deals of an almost exclusively illicit nature that often ended in people getting whacked. While Trump ended up getting into his own illegal schemes, he hasn't yet reverted to the techniques of a true Don and started ordering hits on people, at least not yet.

From his signature grin to his fashionable, tailored Armani suits, Gotti's presence and style would become a point of inspiration for TV and movie stylists all throughout that decade. From *Casino* to *Goodfellas* and even to comedy movies like *Analyze This*, the tailoring, mannerisms, and body language, the "eewws," the "eeyys," and the "stugotses" all came from, and were recirculated within, the tumble-dry cycle of mainstream culture. If you've ever walked into a sandwich shop and seen a *gabagool* sandwich on the menu, you've already experienced this phenomenon, which traces its roots to the 1990s Mafia fascination.

Johnny "Sack" Sacrimoni is one of those *Sopranos* characters who fans can't help but identify with. Head of the Lupertazzi family, he seems like a pretty nice guy with a mostly even-tempered demeanor, while his classic style clearly comes from the Gotti model. Always in nice suits and never with too much hair product, like wannabes Silvio Dante and Paulie Walnuts, Johnny Sack is a pretty straightforward guy who favors an elegant, classic manner of dress.

We say that he's *mostly* even-tempered, though: As *Sopranos* fans will remember, when Ralph "Ralphie" Cifaretto makes an unkind joke about his wife's weight, Johnny Sack goes completely *pazzo* on him, all the way to the point where he nearly orders a hit on Ralphie. Only upon discovering that his sweet, plus-sized Ginny has been stashing candy does Johnny Sack decide to call off the job.

Though Johnny Sack might have dressed similarly to him, real mafioso John Gotti was not such a nice guy, and he was far more flashy and attention-craving—characteristics that would ultimately bring him down. While the relationship between the DeCavalcante family and the Gambino family predates Gotti taking power in 1986, once Gotti assumed control of the organization, he found a friend in DeCavalcante family boss John Riggi.

Gotti and Riggi were said to have had a close, personal relationship, so much so that when Gotti had an itch that he needed scratched, Riggi would jump at the opportunity to help his fellow wiseguy out. While Riggi would bend over backward for Gotti, these favors were not often returned.

The relationship between the Gambino family and the DeCavalcante family was defined by the same patronage-based systems and codes that Sicilian immigrants imported with them to America when they first arrived. While there was a mutual respect, and the DeCavalcantes had their autonomy recognized and validated by the Gambinos and the other member organizations of the Five Families, there was still a clear power imbalance between the larger, more organized crime syndicate and the smaller, scrappy Jersey-born-and-bred roughneck crew.

Riggi's approach to working together with Gotti was diplomatic and even amicable, but their relationship was still one that was maintained by making a lot of concessions, placing the DeCavalcante family at the clearly defined lower tier that they'd always occupied. Gotti still continued to refer to Riggi's guys as "our farm team" (Zambito, 2015, para. 15), and toward the latter part of the 1980s, Gotti would begin to encroach more heavily on the autonomy of the DeCavalcante family.

Anthony Rotondo, the loud-mouthed rat and the guy whose juicy gossip sent gay mobster John D'Amato to an early grave, testified in court, saying that around the time that his father, Vincent "Jimmy" Rotondo, was gunned down in 1988, Gotti started to close in on the family. Suggesting that the DeCavalcante family under Riggi had previously been loyal to the Genovese family, Rotondo observed that the Gambinos, under new capo John Gotti, had expressed a strong desire to claim the DeCavalcante family as their own.

Speaking of a meeting between Riggi and Gotti that took place in the funeral home after his father's death, Rotondo further testified that Riggi was "white as a sheet" after emerging from this sit-down (Zambito, 2015, para. 19), during which Gotti had allegedly informed Riggi that some changes were to be made: The DeCavalcante family would now officially fly under the flag of the Gambino crime family.

In the spring of 1988, John D'Amato was serving as the liaison between Gotti and the DeCavalcante family, a role previously held by Rotondo's father, Vincent, until he was gunned down. During the summer of that year, D'Amato regularly met with Gambino boss John Gotti at the Ravenite Social Club in Manhattan. It's believed that it was during one of these meetings that Gotti learned of the induction practices that the DeCavalcante family had been using.

Instead of using the traditional method of pricking the inductee's finger, dripping their blood on a saint's image, burning the image, and reciting a verbal oath, the DeCavalcante family only observed the verbal oath part of the ceremony. In foregoing any of the blood rituals and occult-like imagery that still tied LCN induction ceremonies to *benedecaria*, the traditional Catholic folk-magic rituals practiced in Southern Italy and most prevalently in Sicily, the DeCavalcantes opted for a more casual, modern approach to inducting guys into their fold.

Upon hearing about these reforms from D'Amato, Gotti was disappointed. Anthony Rotondo was summoned for a talk with Riggi, who expressed concern about DeCavalcante family members leaking secrets to the Gambinos. According to Rotondo, Riggi suspected that it was D'Amato who leaked the insider info on the current induction practices of the family. Vinny Ocean Palermo, who was a soldier under Rotondo at the time, fingered another guy in the leak, fellow DeCavalcante soldier Daniel Annunziata.

Whoever it was that leaked the induction procedure, Riggi, wanting to stay on good terms with ever-encroaching Gotti, ordered that a significant portion of the DeCavalcante family be reinducted. Two reinduction ceremonies were carried out in 1988 in the basement of a New Jersey residence and were presided over by John Riggi, Stefano Vitabile, and longtime captain Paolo "Paul" Farina ("DeCavalcante Family Re-Induction Ceremonies," 2018).

Gotti was a details guy, some might even say a micromanager, as evident in this fuss over the specifics of DeCavalcante induction practices. While it's not known what the motivation behind the moves he made was in trying to claim the DeCavalcantes as his own, it may have its roots in a feud with Genovese family boss

Vincent "The Chin" Gigante. He was a sworn enemy of John Gotti and had even attempted to carry out a hit on the "Teflon Don."

Whether the reason behind Gotti trying to claim the DeCavalcante family as his own was based on the animosity held between Gigante and himself, or if there was some other strategic motivation behind the move, it's evident in his conversations with Riggi and his weighing-in on the specifics of DeCavalcante initiation practices that Gotti had his finger wrapped tightly around the Jersey-based family from the late 1980s onward.

The Genovese Dilemma

Vincent "The Chin" Gigante, John Gotti's enemy, was a former boxer and the leader of the Genovese family who, since 1969, had feigned being insane to avoid serving additional time in prison for his 1959 conviction for dealing heroin. Stumbling around Greenwich Village in a bathrobe once out on parole, Gigante managed to convince law enforcement for 30 years that he was batshit crazy.

Imagine the scene in the Season 5 *Sopranos* episode when Junior Soprano, in an Alzheimer's-induced escapade, manages to drive away in his bathrobe and take off on foot for a tour of his old New Jersey stomping ground in the North Ward of Newark. Later detained by police while crossing the Clay Street Bridge, Junior is returned to his house, where concerned Janice Soprano and Bobby Bacala are tasked with letting Tony know the unfortunate news that their uncle's mental faculties are slipping away.

Junior's dementia-inspired meanderings are just the type of thing that real-life mobster Vincent Gigante would do every day, but in his case, it was all a sham: Gigante knew that if he was found to be insane, he wouldn't be hauled back to prison. This led to him gaining the nicknames "The Oddfather" and the "Enigma in the Bathrobe" by the press. While he continued to pretend to be insane, Gigante was actually still fully capable of running things, staying on as leader of the Genovese family until he passed away in 2005.

Though the exact involvement and extent of Genovese influence on DeCavalcante business up until Gotti tried to seize control of the group are unclear, what is known is that once Gotti got locked up in 1992, Gigante was either self-declared or externally labeled as the "boss of all bosses," even though that official title hadn't been around since the 1931 murder of Salvatore Maranzano. If this suggests that DeCavalcante interests were back in the playing field of the Genovese family, the timing of this play would have put the Genovese family at an advantage, with John D'Amato recently whacked and both Riggi and Gotti on their way to prison.

The details of whether Gigante leveraged the power vacuum that ruptured within the DeCavalcante family in 1992 is unclear, as evidence suggests that Riggi remained loyal to his pal John Gotti and the Gambinos. What is known for certain is that the Genovese family had long controlled the Bayonne waterfront and the longshoremen's union, and the DeCavalcante family would often pop up in dealings within these areas of Mafia business throughout their history.

The unions in the Bayonne Military Ocean Terminal were controlled by a made guy from the Genovese family named John DiGilio—that is, until law enforcement cracked down on their activity at the ports and brought DiGilio and a few other members up on racketeering charges. Though DiGilio was able to beat the charges, the other guys got locked up, and this was ultimately what led to the Gambinos being able to come in and take things over down at the docks (Rocco & Schofield, 2021). Though from all appearances the Genovese family had lost the longshoremen's union to the Gambinos, the DeCavalcante family would benefit from uninterrupted involvement in waterfront union activity thanks to their amicable partnerships with both families.

Recent-day *caporegime* Charlie Stango was said to maintain good relations and had a number of connections with the Genovese family (Rocco & Schofield, 2021) that likely remained in place up until he was brought up on charges in 2015 and got put away 2 years later.

While Stango was overall in good standing with the Genovese family, with the Gambinos there was no choice. He was forced to abide by the pre-existing ties and obligations that preceded him. Since Riggi's meeting with John Gotti back in the late 1980s, the DeCavalcante family's reliance on and loyalty to the larger New York family was basically set in stone.

Stango seemed equally blunt in his resentment, as he was firm in his reluctant acceptance that the DeCavalcante family had essentially become a Gambino satellite. As far as his connections with other New York outfits, including the Lucchese and Colombo families, they continued to remain strong.

Stango's Dealings With the Lucchese and Colombo Families

DeCavalcante *caporegime* Charlie Stango was said to have been close with Ralph V. Perna, the former Lucchese capo who was in charge of all the family's New Jersey operations. Ralph Perna's son, Joseph "Little Joe" Perna, was also a pal to the Vegas-based DeCavalcante captain. In his book *Giovanni's Ring*, undercover agent Giovanni Rocco described an encounter with Little Joe Perna in unflattering terms: "Perna was tall and lanky, but he looked more like a used car salesman than a mob boss. Despite the unprepossessing appearance, I knew him to be a Lucchese heavy" (Rocco & Schofield, 2021, p. 73).

Little Joe Perna made headlines in 2020 for assaulting the ex-husband of one of the stars of *The Real Housewives of New Jersey*, Dina Cantin, and, 10 years earlier, was under the eye of state investigators for income and savings irregularities. Little Joe and his brother, John Perna, were both made as Lucchese soldiers in his Toms River, New Jersey, home back in 2007. Also operating frequently in Toms River was Charlie Stango's crew, including his son Anthony, so it can be assumed that they were all well-acquainted neighbors with many overlapping interests.

Ralph V. Perna, along with his 2 sons, Little Joe and John Perna, were locked up in 2016 on illegal gambling charges, receiving sentences of 8–10 years. A total of 34 guys had been charged in the 2010 indictment that led to their convictions. The Feds alleged that

Perna and his 2 sons were the masterminds behind a gambling ring of staggering scale, with around $2.2 billion in wagers placed over the course of a 15-month investigation (Santolo, 2016). All 3 men pleaded guilty and were sent away.

The Colombo family was another connection during Stango's tenure as remote captain of his New Jersey-based DeCavalcante crew. Once undercover agent Giovanni Rocco infiltrated Stango's crew, he discovered that what was initially thought to be just an investigation targeting Elizabeth-based drug dealer James "Jimmy Smalls" Heeney was turning into a full-scale operation in which other LCN families were now implicated.

Describing a meeting that took place between members of the crew he infiltrated and the Colombo family about a proposal to collaborate on a shipping scheme, Giovanni Rocco discovered a live link between the family that Joe Profaci had started and the present-day DeCavalcante organization. Though the relationship with the Colombos had been rocky in the early days of the Elizabeth–Newark family, things had now come full circle, and they were now shown to be open to forgetting old rivalries and working toward common interests.

Rotondo's Bonanno Family Encounter

The Bonanno family's connections to the DeCavalcante family represented yet another uncovered trove of information that stemmed from the courtroom testimony of noted rat Anthony Rotondo. Though not necessarily useful in helping prosecutors form their cases against the criminals, some of the more anecdotal passages from the courtroom testimony give us some insight into the social relations between different families.

Supposedly, one day Rotondo had visited a Staten Island amusement park and spotted Bonanno family capo Richard "Shellackhead" Cantarella. Upon glancing at each other and sizing each other up, both knew that the other guy was a wiseguy. Big-mouthed Rotondo decided to break the ice and went ahead striking up a conversation with Cantarella, knowing that they were sure to have some mutual connections and business interests.

Sensing that Cantarella might be a Bonanno guy, Rotondo decided to make a bold move, asking if he knew Anthony "T.G." Graziano, another Bonanno capo who Rotondo had an interest in meeting. Cantarella responded that he knew the guy, but since it would have been breaking protocol for him to come out and say directly that he knew him through their "business" connections, he simply responded, "yeah," that he knew the guy. Cantarella fired back, asking if Rotondo knew Danny Annunziata (Capeci, 2005), a Staten Island DeCavalcante captain who owned a few fitness clubs and lived in a four-million-dollar mansion (Smith, 2003).

The two guys, having a chance encounter at the amusement park that day, had to find a way to get around the strict codes of intrafamily introductions, so they arranged for Graziano to introduce them to each other (even though they had already met at the amusement park that day). Only then was Rotondo allowed to introduce his new pal to Annunziata (Capeci, 2005).

These types of rules in communication and respecting the hierarchies involved in making introductions between different

New York and New Jersey crime families exhibit the difficulty that even high-ranking members had establishing dialogue and working relationships with mobbed-up guys from other families. These formalities, however, did not prevent these two families from working together, as evident in the involvement of DeCavalcante associates in an investment scheme that'll seem familiar to any *Sopranos* fan.

The King of Wall Street

Christopher Moltisanti's pump-and-dump scheme in Season 2 of *The Sopranos* gives us a great example of how white-collar mob schemes work. After paying a professional to sit the stockbroker exam in his place, Chrissy is installed as head of a small investment firm and, along with DiMeo family associate Matt Bevilaqua, begins a predatory campaign on unwitting investors.

Encouraging prospective investors to buy large amounts of stock in a company called Webistics—thereby artificially inflating the stock's value—Moltisanti and Bevilaqua are able to rake in a ton of easy money for their family. This is a classic securities-fraud scheme, and once the clueless investors' buying spree elevates the share price of the worthless company, the scammers pull the rug out from under them, dumping massive amounts of their own shares of the stock at a profit and leaving the other investors as bagholders of shares that hold little to no value.

As it turns out, Christopher and Matt's fictional portrayal of this type of white-collar mob scheme had a real-life basis. The Bonanno family, along with members of the Colombo family and some DeCavalcante associates, pulled a similar scam under a company called DMN Capital Investments. DMN was run by Bonanno captain Robert "Little Robert" Lino.

Lino used his company to prey on unsavvy, often elderly investors. Together with Colombo family associate Frank Persico, who like Chris Moltisanti had "passed" the stockbroker exam, Lino masterminded a scheme in which they ran different crews within the cubicles of various investment brokerages in the New York area.

When they finally got busted in 2000, it was one of the biggest securities-fraud cases ever, including 120 defendants across 23 different states (Martin, 2000). The scope and scale of this bust were so large that it even got the attention of the U.S. House of Representatives' Subcommittee on Finance and Hazardous Materials in Commerce.

In a September 13, 2000, session, the minutes of this subcommittee's meeting reveal the level of seriousness with which the government was approaching these issues. They also provide some insight into the government's acknowledgment of the clear connections with current popular-culture entertainment, explicitly mentioning the similarities of these incidents of securities fraud to *The Sopranos*. Former U.S. representative from the 4th district of Ohio Mike Oxley put it like this in his opening statement at the subcommittee's session:

Today's hearing might sound like an episode of *The Sopranos*, but it is not HBO. It is real. We are going to hear the true stories about people getting bilked out of their hard-earned money by the Mob. I know from my own experience as a special agent in the FBI that the Mob will go wherever a dollar is being made. Today that is Wall Street. So it is really not surprising that organized crime is trying to suck some of the life out of the blossoming securities markets. The M-O-B has gone back to school and gotten an MBA. The wiseguys are getting smart. They used to play ponies. Now they are playing the markets and investors for everything they are worth. (U.S. Government Printing Office, 2000, section iii, para. 5)

In his opening statement to the subcommittee meeting, Oxley is justified in drawing the *Sopranos* connection, but the Republican House representative fails to acknowledge that the "blossoming securities market" he describes was already being milked and pilfered by a bunch of nonaffiliated crooks, who, just like mob guys, were trying to make a dime at the expense of ignorant investors they scammed, manipulated, and shook down. At the time, penny-stock pump-and-dump schemes were prevalent throughout the world of finance (think of Jordan Belfort and Danny Prush's predatory penny-stock phone sales campaign as portrayed in the film *The Wolf of Wall Street*). The line between legality and criminality was often skirted in a similar way by both mafiosi and nonconnected finance guys alike.

While the massive Mafia investing scheme around DMN Capital Investments that got busted up in 2000 had participants from a few different mob families, this type of white-collar Mafia crime was said to have been pioneered by one guy in particular, a DeCavalcante family *caporegime* named Philip Abramo, who came to be known as "The King of Wall Street." Like Jordan Belfort, the real-life finance guy whose saga is chronicled in the film *The Wolf of Wall Street*, Philip Abramo was an expert in microcap-stock fraud, and he used the same methods as finance guys use to funnel profits into their own personal wealth to pad the coffers of the DeCavalcante family.

Not only showing that the "greed is good" mentality that was prevalent from the late 1980s up until the 2000 dotcom crash was not exclusive to traditional investment banker types, the fact that Mafia families participated in driving the hype around internet stocks also shows that, rather than stubbornly relying on their historical core business interests, Mafia activity can be very connected to trends in culture. While the mainstay interests of mafiosi often center around extortion, bribery, union racketeering, drugs, and street crime, the DeCavalcante family, along with the other members of the Five Families, was smart enough to adapt and jump on the dotcom craze on the cusp of Y2K, demonstrating that while their traditions may have extended back to the old world, their present-day concerns were very much grounded in contemporary reality.

Even in the same moment that the DeCavalcante family was facing unprecedented pressure—both internally and externally while facing the dual threats of media and law enforcement attention brought on by the foolish escapades of members and associates and a wave of rats within their ranks—their participation in this type of high-level scheming in the equity markets demonstrates that they were well positioned to continue into the 21st century and beyond. Marking a departure from the traditional ways of earning, through Abramo, new higher-ups in the family and those still working their way up the ranks now had a model to start incorporating technology and digital tools into their arsenal of weapons, which until this point, were firmly rooted in the 20th century and even further back in history.

CHAPTER 6
THE PHILADELPHIA CONNECTION

The origins and current-day state of organized crime in New Jersey can't be discussed without mentioning the role that the DeCavalcante family played in the Greater Philadelphia area throughout the 20th century and into today.

Back when Simone "Sam the Plumber" DeCavalcante began solidifying his namesake family into a force to be reckoned with across the region, another capo, Angelo Bruno, was doing the same down in Philadelphia. Pulling the Philadelphia crime family into a more organized and powerful threat, Bruno, like DeCavalcante, would also make such an impact on his family that he'd lend them his name. The family is still known today as the Bruno crime family.

Sam the Plumber and Angelo Bruno

Bruno and DeCavalcante were allies, and as they pulled together their respective crews, modernizing them and making them ready to face the challenges that the mid-20th century brought on, they began engaging in various collaborations that would bolster the standing of both groups in the areas where they had interests. They engaged in a variety of activities together, such as racketeering, extortion, and money laundering, which helped to bring in large sums of cash for both families.

Bruno became one of the most powerful and influential mob bosses in the Philadelphia area during the 20th century. First rising to power in the 1950s, he went on to lead the Philadelphia crime family until he got whacked in 1980. Bruno's rise to power was characterized by his ability to navigate the complex and ever-changing world of organized crime. He was a skilled strategist and a master of political manipulation, and he was able to build a strong and loyal following among the other members of the Philadelphia crime family.

One of Bruno's key strategies was to focus on building alliances with other criminal organizations, in both Philadelphia and other cities. He was able to establish strong relationships with other mob bosses, which helped to increase the power and influence of the Philadelphia crime family and ensured dependence on Sam the Plumber as his main ally in the region. As their respective influence grew in Philadelphia and New Jersey, Bruno and DeCavalcante began to work together more closely, forming a number of partnerships that would help to solidify their position in the criminal underworld.

Despite their close alliance, there were also tensions between the two men. Bruno was known for his ruthless tactics and his willingness to use violence to achieve his goals while DeCavalcante was more of a behind-the-scenes operator who preferred to keep a low profile. This led to some personal conflicts, as they had different ideas about how to run their criminal enterprises. Despite these tensions, however, the alliance between Bruno and DeCavalcante was relatively strong, and it continued for many years. They were both respected and feared figures in the criminal world, and their names were synonymous with organized crime in New Jersey and the Greater Philadelphia area.

In addition to his political acumen, Bruno, like DeCavalcante, was known for his ability to keep a low profile and avoid attracting too much attention from law enforcement. Bruno was also known for avoiding unnecessary violence, lending him the nickname "The Gentle Don."

One of the most notable things about Bruno's tenure as mob boss was the way he reformed the traditional organized-crime model. He introduced new systems for sharing information and coordinating criminal activities, and he worked to improve communication and collaboration among the different crews and factions within the organization. This approach helped keep the Philadelphia crime family out of the spotlight and allowed it to operate more quietly and efficiently than other crime families.

Despite his efforts to keep a low profile and avoid drawing attention from law enforcement, Bruno's reign as mob boss came to an end when he was murdered in 1980. His death marked the end of an era for the Philadelphia crime family, and it marked the beginning of a new phase in the history of organized crime in the city.

One of the most significant collaborations between the two men was their involvement in the construction industry. Both DeCavalcante and Bruno had strong ties to labor unions, and they used this to their advantage by controlling the flow of contracts and labor in the construction industry. They also used their influence to extort money from contractors and developers, which helped to further increase their wealth and power.

As the decades passed and the criminal landscape changed, their partnership eventually began to unwind a bit. Bruno was murdered in 1980, and DeCavalcante, of course, would be arrested and imprisoned several years later.

Don't Shoot the Messenger

The relationship between the Bruno family and the DeCavalcante family continued even once Bruno was out of the picture and Sam the Plumber got locked away. With John Riggi heading up the DeCavalcantes and Nicodemo "Little Nicky" Scarfo placed in charge of the Philly mob after Bruno got whacked, the two groups continued the connections established under the successful tenures of DeCavalcante and Bruno.

However, Scarfo's different approach would lead to some tensions between the two bosses. Unlike Bruno—who like Sam the Plumber was respected for his measured, diplomatic approach—Scarfo became famous for his violent and ruthless tactics, and his reign as mob boss was marked by a high level of violence and chaos within the organization.

Although his tenure was marked by an uptick in violence and disorder, Scarfo managed to maintain a close working relationship with DeCavalcante boss John Riggi. The two men had known each other for many years, and they had mutual respect for each other's abilities as mob bosses. The partnership between Scarfo and Riggi was built on a foundation of mutual benefit.

Scarfo was able to use the DeCavalcante crime family's connections and resources in New Jersey to expand the reach and influence of the Philadelphia crime family while Riggi was able to use Scarfo's connections and resources in Philadelphia to solidify the grip that New Jersey's original born-and-bred family had on its own turf. The two men also worked together on a variety of criminal undertakings, such as racketeering, extortion, and money laundering. They were able to use their combined resources and connections to generate large sums of money, which helped to bolster the financial positions of both families.

Although they had a relatively close partnership, there were tensions beginning to grow between Scarfo and Riggi. Scarfo's often violent and ruthless tactics brought unwanted attention from law enforcement while Riggi was more of a behind-the-scenes operator who preferred to keep a low profile. This difference in leadership style led to some conflicts between the two men, as they had different ideas about how to manage their criminal enterprises. Despite these tensions, however, the partnership between Scarfo and Riggi remained solid, and it continued until they both got implicated in some legal trouble.

Riggi was arrested and imprisoned in the 1990s, and Scarfo was also arrested and imprisoned a few years later. While their respective families put in the extra effort to operate as normal with both guys behind bars, they were never able to achieve the same level of power and influence or attain the same level of collaboration as they did with their bosses walking free.

That said, Scarfo was notorious enough to lend his name to his Philly mob group, and the Bruno family from this point onward would often be referred to as the Bruno–Scarfo crime family. The fact that he was dealt a life sentence for murder and racketeering would not deter him from continuing to run the family from behind bars.

Once Little Nicky got sent away, his son, Nicodemo "Nicky" Scarfo Jr. became both Scarfo and Riggi's messenger, passing orders and messages back and forth between the Philly and Jersey mob bosses and their respective underbosses and crews.

Nicky Jr. continued in this role until John Riggi and Scarfo Sr. were caught running their crime families from federal prison, and they were charged along with 37 other alleged mobsters in a state racketeering conspiracy indictment. The prosecutors alleged that Scarfo Sr. controlled Bruno–Scarfo dealings for 3.5 years while behind bars with the aid of Scarfo Jr., who managed communications between the boss and his crews on the outside. Besides Scarfo and Scarfo Jr., other top-ranking members of the Bruno–Scarfo family, including Joseph "Scoops" Licata, were also indicted in the proceedings. The cases against both Riggi and Scarfo were based upon some highly incriminating evidence that was presented in court: hundreds of conversations that were secretly taped by mob informant George Fresolone (*The Press of Atlantic City*, 2015).

Scarfo Sr., who was already serving multiple long prison terms that equated to a life sentence, remained behind bars until he passed away in January 2017 at a federal medical facility. Unlike Riggi, Scarfo would never walk a free man again.

Though DeCavalcante boss John Riggi was released from prison in 2012, he passed away in 2015, living out the last few years of his life Junior Soprano-style in a modest house in Edison, New Jersey. With a nurse by his side to care for the ailing mobster during his last days, Riggi was already past the point of being able to lead in any capacity.

For six years, the family's operations had already been in the hands of the Sicilian Francesco Guarracci, who was proving himself to be largely capable, and he would continue the DeCavalcantes' allyship with the Bruno–Scarfo family.

Today, the state of Pennsylvania is still seeking to seize the assets, equities, and real estate holdings that were related to other criminal activities in the web of crime that the Bruno–Scarfo family, together with the DeCavalcante family and New York's Five Families, spread across the Philadelphia and South Jersey regions during Scarfo's rule. Moreover, the area remains a hotbed for Mafia activity, with members of the DeCavalcante family and other Mafia families still active within the region, especially in South Jersey, home of Atlantic City.

Atlantic City

One of the most significant areas of operation for the Bruno–Scarfo crime family has been Atlantic City, New Jersey, which is known as the "Vegas of the East Coast," thanks to its thriving casino and tourism industry. The Bruno–Scarfo family has maintained a number of interests in the city, including casinos and other businesses. Working closely with other organized-crime groups in the area, the Philly-based mob group has continued to exert their influence across a wide range of illegal activities in the area.

The Bruno–Scarfo family along with the DeCavalcante family and New York's Five Families represent a powerful alliance that still controls much of Atlantic City and the surrounding areas even today. A December 2020 federal indictment of 15 guys from the Bruno–Scarfo family names loansharking, bookmaking, and drug trafficking as their main businesses in the Atlantic City area.

One of the key ways in which the Bruno crime family and their allies have been able to exert control over the city is through their control of the labor unions that work in the casinos and other businesses. By controlling the unions, they are able to control the flow of contracts and labor, which has given them a significant advantage over their competitors.

In a U.S. government lawsuit in 1990 against an Atlantic City casino workers' union, Little Nicky Scarfo, with the aid of his son Nicky Jr., was named as the alleged union boss. The Bruno crime family and their allies used their influence and control of the unions to extort money from casino owners, developers, and other businesses in Atlantic City. They would threaten violence or other forms of intimidation if their demands were not met, allowing them to generate large sums of money through illegal activities.

Despite their efforts to keep a low profile and avoid drawing attention from law enforcement, the Bruno crime family and their allies were not able to dodge the attention of law enforcement. In the 1980s and 1990s, a number of high-profile investigations targeted the family and their allies, and many members were arrested and imprisoned.

CHAPTER 7
THE FAMILY TODAY

Cocaine

Cocaine trafficking and distribution, in particular, has been a major source of income for the DeCavalcante crime family in recent years. The organization has been known to import large quantities of the drug from South America and funnel it through an extended distribution network that spans much of the East Coast. The DeCavalcante family also continues to utilize their extensive network of legitimate-seeming business fronts and their Rolodex of associates to launder the proceeds of their drug trafficking activities. The family has been able to maintain its grip on the cocaine trade through its use of violence and intimidation. They've been known to use brutal tactics to silence rivals and maintain control over their territory.

In the past, the DeCavalcante family along with the Five Families and the Bruno–Scarfo family have also been known to use their political and law enforcement connections to protect their operations. While many of these connections eroded following large corruption scandals and large-scale busts that threatened to end these families for good, the crime families still benefit from the strongholds they exert at the major ports in the area.

Despite the efforts of law enforcement agencies to disrupt the DeCavalcante crime family's cocaine trafficking and distribution operations, the organization has been able to adapt and continue operating uninterrupted. This is partly due to their ability to infiltrate legitimate businesses and use them as fronts for their illegal activities.

Though the DeCavalcante family has been largely successful in keeping the majority of their drug operations under wraps, there have been a few recent incidents in particular that have brought their doings to light, once again bringing the unwanted attention of law enforcement.

On the Waterfront

In February 2019, 3,200 pounds of cocaine were seized at Port Newark. Though the authorities declined to name the suspected individuals or organizations behind the bust, it's well known that one or a consortium of the local Mafia families had knowledge of the shipping container it arrived in.

Down at the docks, the Mafia is still in charge, and this is something that modern-day Mafia crime families have to their advantage. Though they may be less sophisticated and less organized than their Chinese and Russian counterparts, traditional LCN Mafia families have the advantage of their firm grip on waterfront unions and operations. The DeCavalcante family, the Five Families, and the Bruno–Scarfo family all have guys planted within the ranks of dockworkers, inspectors, and other positions, not just at Port Newark but also at all of the other smaller ports and shipping container terminals throughout the New York and New Jersey area.

Giving LCN families a competitive advantage over the arrivals and departures of almost all contraband in the area, their command and influence down at the ports give them the upper hand when it comes to the traffic of illegal goods of all kinds.

While the presence of all local Mafia families is widespread throughout the area, it's been said that, today, the Genovese family still exerts the most influence over what goes down on the New Jersey side (Ford, 2019). If this assertion is true, it would mean that the Genovese family managed to wrangle control back from the encroaching Gambinos during John Gotti's time. While the Genoveses had traditionally maintained control of the longshoremen's union at the Bayonne Military Ocean Terminal, it was said that, during Gotti's reign, control of this important strategic zone was lost by the Genovese family to the Gambinos.

So, whether control of the Jersey-side port operations was held continuously by the Genovese or the encroaching Gambinos of the 1990s were able to wrest power and hold it for some time, it can be assumed that the DeCavalcante family has benefited from uninterrupted access to the port and longshoremen's union, as they've continued maintaining good relations with both of these families throughout modern times.

Dealing and Distribution

The strategic positioning and presence of all LCN families at the ports have undoubtedly benefited the DeCavalcante family in their import operations. But, as far as their distribution of illicit goods once they arrive, not much is known, except for the glimmers of insights gained the few times that the long arm of the law has managed to crack open the vault of secrecy in recent years.

In 2015, 10 members of the DeCavalcante family, including Charlie Stango and Anthony Stango, were charged with conspiracy to distribute cocaine, along with a plethora of other charges related to murder plots and prostitution operations that the father and son team had been planning. While Stango's crew was based mostly down in Toms River, another DeCavalcante crew up in Elizabeth was charged at the same time for conspiracy to distribute more than 500 grams of cocaine. Two DeCavalcante guys, James Heeney and Rosario Pali, from the Elizabeth drug ring had been captured making incriminating statements on recordings made by undercover officers and had even sold drugs to undercover officers.

As for Charlie Stango and his son, Anthony, a murder plot was what garnered them the attention that would eventually lead to them being brought up on charges. Thinking that they were contracting a hit out to a motorcycle gang, Stango ordered the hit through an undercover agent and, in doing so, made it inevitable that he'd be taken down. It was revealed that Stango had sought the approval of DeCavalcante consigliere Frank Nigro and other high-ranking members to carry out the hit, which was to be on a rival member, Luigi "The Dog" Oliveri. In 2017, Stango was sentenced to 10 years in federal prison for plotting to murder Oliveri over the phone from his Nevada hideout.

With the roundup complete, the DeCavalcante family had again been caught up in a large-scale federal case that brought unwanted attention to their organization and their doings. That said, it didn't deter the family members who evaded charges from continuing their many businesses. With Guarraci having passed away the previous year and Charles "Big Ears" Majuri now occupying the highest seat, the show had to go on, including the distribution and sales of illegal drugs. The drug trade was simply too profitable to give up, and while there wouldn't be any big busts in the next few years, lower-level DeCavalcante guys would continue to face charges related to this illicit trade.

In April 2021, Jason Vella, a Toms River DeCavalcante associate who was likely part of Charlie Stango's crew before Stango got sent packing, was found guilty of cocaine possession with intent to distribute and sentenced to 15 months in federal prison. Two years before, he was arrested during an authorized search of his home, where 150 grams of cocaine, various types of drug paraphernalia, large quantities of cash, and jewelry were found (Larsen, 2021).

So, while in recent years, the DeCavalcante crime family has faced increased pressure from law enforcement agencies, their operations continue strong in the thriving area of drug trafficking and sales. And even though several high-ranking members of the organization have been arrested and convicted of various crimes related to drug trafficking and distribution, the DeCavalcante crime family continues to be a major player in the cocaine trade on the East Coast.

Prostitution

Aside from his pioneering ventures into Mafia "smart working" as the first remotely based DeCavalcante capo, sending orders to his Toms River-based crew from outside Las Vegas, Charlie Stango also had some big ideas in another area: the sex trade. The problem was, however, that he revealed these plans to an undercover agent and managed to blow his plans for the high-end bordello and call service he dreamed of creating.

Maybe it was all that time Stango was spending out in the Nevada desert, where prostitution had already been legally sanctioned since 1971, but for whatever reason, Stango was inspired to dream big by putting a luxury brothel in the town of Toms River. However, Stango would soon find that his dreams of breaking into the sex industry were bigger than his britches, and in planning to realize his scheme, Stango unknowingly ended up leaking the details of his plans to an undercover agent through a phone wiretap.

Stango's brothel, which was to be marketed as a luxury escort service, was intended to cater to wealthy white-collar workers. Partnering with a pair of local women, who are unnamed in the 2015 Department of Justice criminal complaint, and his son, Anthony, Stango had plans for this business to bolster his own wealth, as well as the coffers of the DeCavalcante family. The plan was that Anthony and the Toms River crew would be in charge of managing this business.

Suggesting that the guys set up a real club to serve as a front for the operation, Stango even gave some input on the beverage offerings, pointing out that if they kept drink prices low it could drive more "legitimate" revenue. Another idea of the ever-entrepreneurial capo was to run a veteran charity scam out of the club, distributing promotional materials for a charity that supported wounded veterans but, in reality, would go straight into bank accounts associated with the DeCavalcante family.

Anthony Stango, taking on the role as manager of the brothel project, was also recorded making incriminating statements about the business operation. Claiming that he had already secured 12 women in New Jersey willing to provide their services at the Toms River brothel, he also had 5 women in New York City and an additional 8 in Philadelphia. When his pops inquired about how he was going to manage all of those girls across the different locations, Anthony said that he already had a plan in place and that there was going to be a website put up offering outcall services.

Though the Toms River brothel was to be marketed as a luxury service, Anthony made it clear that he had plans to serve all types of clientele, noting in a wiretapped phone call to his dad, "I got 'em all sizes and colors, all prices. I got cheapies that you gotta pay me 100 an hour for… gotta give you a $30 fucking blowjob, and then I got fucking broads that you're gonna pay me 350 to 500 an hour" (United States of America v. Stango, 2015, p. 31).

While Charlie and Anthony were talking like they were starting to fancy themselves as big-time pimps, the investigators who had been tracking their every move knew that, even with their DeCavalcante family membership, they were little more than small-time crooks. Once the Feds' investigation cracked open Stango's dealings enough to lead to indictments and subsequent convictions, their dreams of opening the VIP brothel in Toms River must have been the furthest thing from their minds.

The Feds began rounding up members of his crew, including Charlie and Anthony Stango themselves. All in all, 15 guys would face charges related to the escort business, the cocaine distribution, as well as the hit that Charlie Stango ordered over the phone on his rival, fellow DeCavalcante member Luigi "The Dog" Oliveri.

Waste Management and Illegal Dumping

Waste management is a business that'll forever be associated with organized crime in New Jersey, so much so that it was highlighted as being the "main gig" of capo Tony Soprano in *The Sopranos*. While he held the official title of "waste management consultant"— and did eventually get a desk at Barone Sanitation to uphold the appearance that he had legitimate sources of income—it's universally understood that when a Jersey guy like Tony mutters that he's in the "waste management business," there's a high likelihood that he's mobbed up.

Although many of these businesses operate as legitimate dumpster haulers for local businesses and contractors, as always with Mafia-run businesses, there's a darker, illegal side to their operations. New Jersey has become somewhat of a safe haven for unscrupulous dumpers, its more lax regulations luring guys who've already been banned from New York across the river to dump illegal, often highly toxic loads of waste.

This kind of illegal dumping, or "dirt brokering," as it's often called has been a big business for the Mafia for some time. Up to the current day, the practices continue to take a toll on the environment and the communities that surround illegal dump sites—often exposing workers and residents to cancer-causing chemicals. The

New Jersey State Commission of Investigation has regularly released reports over the past decade warning that the state has a glaring deficit in resources to enforce the laws around the state's recycling program, leaving regulators and citizens alike powerless against unscrupulous operators, many of whom have ties to organized crime (Star-Ledger Editorial Board, 2019).

These types of schemes have remained widespread throughout the Garden State, but they haven't gone unnoticed by regulators and politicians. The Commission of Investigation's findings did allow prosecutors to carry out two convictions in 2016 related to dirt brokering, one of which charged longtime DeCavalcante member James Castaldo. Castaldo along with associate Gerard Pica had been involved in an extortion racket in which they received cash payments from various contractors and signed off on agreements that funneled tainted landfill materials into a municipal project managed by the Hudson County Improvement Authority. The poison dirt ended up in a nine-hole golf course in Jersey City.

Though the conviction of DeCavalcante member James Castaldo may have slowed down some of the family's illegal dumping schemes for a short period, it's likely that they, along with the Five Families, saw it as just a minor setback and continued with their illegal dumping of hazardous waste.

In 2017, a Bonanno crime family captain was implicated in another dirt-brokering scheme, in which waste from demolition sites that were tainted with toxins and other biological hazards were sold off as fill materials. In this particular case, the poison dirt found its way onto the properties of unwitting landowners whose yards had been eroded during the tidal surge caused by superstorm Sandy. Demonstrating that local mob families have not given up in recent years, and are still up to their business as usual, illegal dumping is still thriving in the Garden State.

In 2019, a New Jersey senate bill attempted to remediate some of the loopholes that allowed many of these illegal dumping schemes to slip through the cracks, adding background checks for waste management operators, expanding testing protocol by the Department of Environmental Protection, allowing law enforcement to take more proactive roles in inspecting trucks and issuing fines, and also making it possible for the state's Attorney General to share information with New York (Star-Ledger Editorial Board, 2019).

Although the bill passed the state senate, it got jammed up in the Assembly and, like many things in New Jersey, got pushed to the back burner, allowing the violations and environmental crimes to continue, giving the DeCavalcante family, along with the Five Families, the mandate to continue their illegal dumping businesses.

The Construction Racket

The construction racket has been at the core of the DeCavalcantes' business operations since the early bootlegging days of the Elizabeth–Newark family, but it wasn't until the reign of John Riggi that the long-held ties between Elizabeth's Laborers' International Union of North America (LIUNA) Local 394 and the crime family would become more firmly cemented.

Through these strong affiliations with Elizabeth-based Local 394, as well as with the Painters District Council No. 30 in Millburn, the DeCavalcante family has continued to exert a strong influence on the New Jersey construction industry. These strong established connections have allowed DeCavalcante members to be placed in consulting and leadership roles within the unions and have granted them access to jobs within local contracting companies.

Although their jobs and leadership positions in unions and construction companies have often been obtained through illegal means of coercion and extortion, DeCavalcante family members throughout history have been noted for their exceptionally strong work ethic. Members and associates have historically taken pride in showing up daily, clocking in and out just like the other working joes who were nonaffiliated. Tom Troncone on Mafia-interest site The Chicago Syndicate noted that "for years, the joke among New York mobsters was that you couldn't have a 'sit-down' with a member of the DeCavalcante crime syndicate until after 4 o'clock. That's when the whistles blew and the job sites closed for the day" (2006, para. 1).

In contrast to the kinds of "no-show" construction and waste management jobs often highlighted in *The Sopranos*, some have argued that, aside from their smaller size, the one thing that has always separated the DeCavalcante family from other local crime families has been their willingness to show up and hold real jobs (Troncone, 2006).

While the period of the late 1980s through the mid-1990s was defined by the more flashy, braggadocious style of bosses like Vinny

Ocean Palermo and wannabe wiseguys like Ralphie Guarino, many DeCavalcante family members were low-key individuals who took pride in their blue-collar union jobs and didn't hold aspirations toward becoming media-friendly John Gotti types.

Although many DeCavalcante members verifiably were hardworking and didn't treat their extorted jobs as opportunities to slack off, there were certainly others that were just clowning around. Rat Anthony Capo, the guy who loaded John D'Amato full of bullets in the back of a car in 1992, testified that he *did* in fact have a "no-show" job like the ones often shown in *The Sopranos*, and that he even collected overtime for this position. The New Jersey State Commission of Investigation pointed to similar patterns of laziness in their assessment of the DeCavalcante family's work ethic, stating in their 2015 report that "DeCavalcante members were often no-shows or did no work at laborers' jobs" (Commission of Investigation, p. 123).

Whether or not members of the family were as hardworking in their legitimate front jobs as some Mafia historians describe—or if they were just calling it in—what is for certain is that higher-ups in the organization were ruthless in their exploitation and leveraging of the unions. Through their control and influence at Local 394, the DeCavalcante family has been able to extort contractors on a wide range of goods, services, and building materials.

Recent-day DeCavalcante boss—Ribera, Sicily, native Francesco Guarraci—was officially a laborer and, later, a foreman with the union. Back in 2006 when he assumed power of the family as acting boss, he was accused of trying to take control of Local 394 from the parent organization of the union and was forced into early "retirement" from his position there. Although Guarraci had the backing of many long-standing DeCavalcante members and had been putting plans into motion with modernizing the Ribera Club, which he had successfully managed since 1989, his move to seize more control over Local 394 was one step too far for outside union watchdogs and officials.

Though it's likely that some DeCavalcante members remained active and influential in Local 394 in the years that followed Guarraci's 2006 ouster from the union, it can be inferred that the last 15 years or so have been marked by a steady decrease in the influence that the family once held over it. The efforts to break up the DeCavalcante family's influence and corruption within Local 394 date all the way back to the mid-1990s, when a joint campaign was initiated between LIUNA and the U.S. Department of Justice.

Before staging the coup against encroaching Guarraci back in 2006, the anticorruption campaign had already led to the permanent ouster of current-day acting boss Charles "Big Ears" Majuri, along with *caporegime* Giuseppe "Pino" Schifilliti. The two DeCavalcante guys were already banned from participating in any union activities within LIUNA, even before Guarraci came into the picture (Commission of Investigation, 2004).

With Majuri the de facto boss of the family today as its oldest surviving member, it's unlikely that DeCavalcante family interests are on the table in any meaningful way at Local 394 anymore. Even if some DeCavalcante members and associates may still be involved in Local 394 or the construction businesses they work with, the wave of anticorruption efforts by LIUNA in conjunction with the U.S. Department of Justice seems to have reduced what was, for many decades, a huge cash flow for the family into a slow trickle.

CHAPTER 8

RATS

Big-Mouthed Rat, Anthony Rotondo

If there's one dirty rat whose courtroom revelations have been marked by their sensationalist, tabloid-friendly content, it's loudmouth DeCavalcante capo Anthony Rotondo. Noted for being college educated—which wasn't exactly common among wiseguys—one thing he clearly wasn't educated in was keeping his mouth shut.

Word on the street was that his father, old-school DeCavalcante mobster Vincent "Jimmy the Gent" Rotondo, had high aspirations for his son, hoping that he'd eventually find a path out of "the life" by getting a college education. Vincent hoped that his son might one day become a lawyer, a sentiment echoed by Rotondo himself once he landed in the courtroom for other reasons, namely for being implicated in the 1989 Fred Weiss murder and for being the guy behind gay mobster John D'Amato getting whacked.

Anthony Rotondo got made as a DeCavalcante soldier in 1982. His father, Vincent, must have been proud of his son, even though he had expressed a desire for Anthony to pursue a legitimate career as a professional. Vincent was the number-two guy in the organization at that time and was highly regarded by his colleagues.

While the 1980s were a prosperous time for the DeCavalcante family, toward the end of the decade, there was an uptick in tension as John Gotti and his Gambino family began to encroach on their businesses and weigh in on interfamily power issues. Aside from these struggles, the late 1980s also brought in a new wave of legal troubles for the family.

Anthony Rotondo's father happened to be one of the guys who was potentially affected by the courtroom struggles of a DeCavalcante associate. Though he was probably regretting it at this time, there was no way to turn back the clock, and Vincent was struggling with issues stemming from the fact that he had brought an outside guy into the family fold, a Long Island dentist named Jesse Hyman, who moonlighted as a loan shark.

Vincent Rotondo's association with the guy was drawing ugly looks from other members of the family's inner circle, as it was looking more and more like Hyman, who was standing trial for loan sharking, was going to cooperate with investigators in an attempt to reduce the 30-year sentence he was looking at. Since Hyman was brought in by Rotondo, Rotondo was viewed as partly responsible for the fallout that would come from this guy who was about to turn rat.

On January 4, 1988, Vincent Rotondo was found behind the wheel of his Lincoln, a container of calamari in his lap and his face blasted by a hail of bullets. The *New York Daily News* noted of the crime scene that "police believe the squid was dinner, not the 'Godfather'-style calling card of the hit man" (Farrell & Capeci, 1988, para. 9). Symbolism devoid or not, a clear message was sent: The

DeCavalcante family had no tolerance for rats, even if they were just associates.

While John Riggi is thought to be the guy who sanctioned the hit on Vincent Rotondo, some have suggested that John Gotti was *really* behind it. It would only be a matter of weeks before the two bosses had that fateful meeting at the funeral home, in which Gotti made it clear to Riggi that the DeCavalcante family was now officially flying under the flag of the Gambinos.

For Anthony Rotondo, the double gut-punch of seeing his father taken out in a violent hit, and being cognizant of the changes sweeping in around the family leadership and hierarchy, must have been a hard thing to digest. But the young mobster carried on, getting moved up to capo himself to pull up the slack left by his father's unfortunate demise.

Becoming a valuable contributor and earner within the family, Rotondo was in many ways a model mobster. But one day, like many previously loyal guys, he would eventually crack and succumb to the lowest thing a mobbed-up guy can do: ratting on his own family.

Rotondo wasn't a dumb guy—having graduated from Nazareth Academy, a private college-preparatory high school and also having obtained a degree in business from St. Francis College in Brooklyn—he was well prepared for the kind of career his father had envisioned for him.

That potential career path as a professional came to an end in 2004 when he found himself on trial, facing life in prison on a variety of charges, including 4 murders, conspiring to carry out 3 additional murders, extortion, robbery, and breaking and entering. While he didn't have to apply all his book learning to commit all these crimes, what he did do once faced with life behind bars was combine his common sense with his knowledge of legal processes.

Making the tough decision to go the way of loan-shark dentist Jesse Hyman, whose loose lips led to Rotondo's father getting his head blasted off on his way back from the fish market that day back in 1988, Anthony Rotondo turned rat, and the revelations of his courtroom testimony and banter went on to convict many other DeCavalcante family members, as well as provide us Mafia enthusiasts with a broad range of insights and insider information about the DeCavalcante family and their operations.

Without the testimony of rats like Anthony Rotondo and other guys who turned, there would be a shortage of the kinds of vivid stories and anecdotes that grace the pages of this book, and also make their way into the Mafia entertainment we've come to love. So, while we hate rats for the fact that they turned on their families, we have to give it up for them and appreciate their contributions to Mafia tales, both true and fictional.

Wannabe Wiseguy Rat, Ralph "Ralphie" Guarino

Another notable rat that plagued the DeCavalcante family wasn't even a made guy himself. Readers will remember Ralphie Guarino as the wannabe wiseguy whose bungled escapades at the World Trade Center left him with fistfuls of difficult-to-launder foreign cash. After Vinny Ocean had already compromised the cover of the low-profile DeCavalcante organization in the mid-1990s through his brash efforts to make the public threat against his strip bar into a civil rights issue, Guarino swooped in just a few years later with his World Trade Center hijinks, which gave the DeCavalcante family further unwanted media attention.

Worse yet, Ralphie went rat. To this day, that's what he'll always be remembered as: a fake, wannabe wiseguy, who was just a low-level associate but thought so highly of himself to flip—electing to wear a wire for the FBI and thereby exposing DeCavalcante family members to government surveillance that would begin causing some serious problems for the organization.

Cigargoyles was the name of Ralphie's place on the East River, right near the Brooklyn Bridge. This cigar club and restaurant tried to capitalize on the cigar craze of the late 1990s, but it would prove to be a challenging investment for the high-rolling, but not highly bank-rolled, crook. Though Ralphie spent a lot of his time earning as a DeCavalcante associate, he also had a taste for the finer things. He relished spending his hard-earned cash on pricy cigars and spoiling himself with spa treatments and manicures; he was known around town for his vanity. Since he loved wrapping himself in luxury and projecting an image that he was living the good life, he decided to take his passion for all the signifiers of the rich and try to funnel it all into his Cigargoyles venture (Smith, 2003).

Cigargoyles was a failed venture so far, and that meant that Ralphie had to seek out a new source of cash. Aside from the financial stresses stemming from his business venture, Ralphie's wallet was being drained by his girlfriend, who liked spending just as much as he did and had a penchant for coaxing her wannabe-wiseguy lover-boy into dropping loads of money on expensive hotels (Smith, 2003).

One day Ralphie got a tip from his trusted friend, Sal Calciano, a guy who had also grown up near the docks of the South Brooklyn waterfront. Sal worked at the World Trade Center and gave Ralphie all the information he needed to pull off a seemingly clear-cut and simple old-time bank heist at a Bank of America branch housed within the Twin Towers.

Although Ralphie Guarino was just a DeCavalcante associate and some considered him to be a bit of a wannabe, he had a pretty impressive resume of criminal activity behind him. Even though he was an aspiring "wiseguy," wisdom seemed to be something he didn't have much of. He would demonstrate this soon by hiring the three stooges of small-time cronies to execute this bozo-headed escapade at the twin towers.

Knowing that the place was surveilled and guarded up the wazoo, Guarino's plan was to contract the job out to some low-life Brooklyn street thugs to avoid catching any flack himself. This smart thinking was something that would later gain him some notoriety with higher-ups in the family, namely with Vincent "Vinny Ocean" Palermo.

On January 9, 1998, it was time for Guarino's cronies to carry out their mission. Armed with forged ID cards and duffel bags that concealed balaclavas and handguns, they were waved on through by a lax security guard, who just glanced at their forged passes, failing to actually scan them to make sure they were really valid. With few other unexpected difficulties, the guys managed to pull off the heist, casually strolling away from the crime scene. Guarino was parked nearby, watching to make sure the guys got out and were making their way to take different subway routes before the planned rendezvous back in Brooklyn (Smith, 2003).

The Feds managed to nab Ralphie just a few days after the robbery, showing up at his Staten Island home for a conversation. Suggesting that they head off to a windowless room at the Manhattan FBI office at Federal Plaza, Ralphie complied and was then interrogated by the agents. Once the agents got to the point of discussing his options, Ralphie's main concern shifted from trying to figure out how the hell to launder the stacks of foreign banknotes with which he was now stuck to trying to save his ass from landing back in the slammer for up to 20 years.

The Feds had collected tons of evidence fingering Ralphie as the mastermind behind the World Trade Center heist, and they used that intel toward threatening him, making it clear that his previous convictions would also play into sentencing and prison terms on any new charges. Ralphie caved in and agreed to wear a wire. So, like Salvatore "Big Pussy" Bonpensiero in *The Sopranos*, he became the guy in the organization who allowed the Feds to peep in and see the inner workings of the DeCavalcante family. But, the Feds wouldn't have such an easy time in doing so.

Also mirroring *The Sopranos*, real-life instances of mob wiretapping often see Feds sifting through a whole bunch of unusable, irrelevant content. Far from a glorified investigative operation, the day-to-day of real Feds is very much as portrayed in *The Sopranos*—lots of sitting around in a van and waiting for minuscule fragments of information that they hope can eventually lead to indictments.

Rat From the Suburbs, Vincent "Vinny Ocean" Palermo

When Vinny Ocean first met Ralphie Guarino, he liked the guy. Even though Ralphie was a low-level wannabe, Vinny knew that it must have taken some balls to pull off the kind of heist that Ralphie was behind at the World Trade Center, and he appreciated that. What he didn't know was that his new friend was wearing a wire, and it wouldn't be long before Vinny Ocean himself would become a rat too.

Up to the point where he came into contact with Ralphie, Vinny Ocean was largely outside the scope of any FBI interest. Though his Wiggles strip club made headlines, and there were whispers that its owner was a mobbed-up guy who lived in a nice suburban Long Island home, the Feds didn't have a good understanding of exactly who was on the DeCavalcante ruling panel at that time. All the Feds knew was that, with John Riggi behind bars, the DeCavalcantes were likely still struggling with the same kind of intrafamily drama that had defined the periods of turbulence that often plagued the family once big capos got locked up.

Vinny decided to move Ralphie up, letting him know that, from then on, he'd be put with his driver Joseph "Joey O" Masella. Vinny hoped that this move would put him at a strategic advantage, being able to keep an eye on the upstart associate by putting him with another guy within his circle.

Though Vinny relied on Masella to shuttle him around, the two had a checkered past. Though they were close friends, they had a brief falling out that stemmed from the attempted hit on Charles "Big

Ears" Majuri that Vinny ordered back when the ruling panel was first formed. Masella, along with Jimmy Gallo and Anthony Capo, were the guys who failed to carry out the hit on Majuri after realizing that there was a state trooper patrol car parked right across the street. After the failed attempt, Vinny still wanted Majuri out of the picture.

Joey O flew down to Florida to share the unfortunate news with Vinny that the hit wasn't going to be carried out, and at first, he was disappointed. Vinny then decided that there were so many other guys in the DeCavalcante family who wanted Majuri out of the picture that the hit may as well be carried out by some other member, some other time.

Ultimately, Vinny decided to let Joey O off the hook for the failed contract he had out on Majuri, and the two remained on good terms. While Joey O was Vinny's trusted driver, and the two were friends, he pissed off Vinny with his irresponsibility, somehow racking up close to half a million dollars in gambling debts. Another point of contention between the two guys was that Vinny suspected that Masella was getting a little too close to the Bruno–Scarfo family.

Aside from the few small problems Vinny had with Masella, he was the perfect companion for wannabe wiseguy and debt-ridden Ralphie Guarino. The two boneheads were in over their heads, and Vinny knew he could hold this over the two guys to keep them in line. What Vinny didn't know, though, was that Ralphie was wired up—and that in moving Ralphie up to go together with Masella, Vinny Ocean was unknowingly opening the floodgates to a whole bunch of information to eventually make its way into the hands of the Feds.

Aside from the unknown factor brewing within Vinny Ocean's crew, with Ralphie starting to distribute FBI wiretapped cell phones around to various members, there was another problem they had on their hands: Ralphie's new companion, Joey O, had just got whacked. Thinking he was being called out to a Brooklyn golf course by a bookmaker who was looking to make good on some money he owed Masella, instead of getting paid off, he got knocked off—by DeCavalcante associate Anthony Greco, another guy tied up in gambling debt.

With Joey O out of the picture, wired-up rat Ralphie Guarino was able to move up. Now more powerful within the crew and free from the watchful eye of Masella, it was only a matter of time before the walls began caving in around Vinny Ocean and his crew.

By 1999, Vinny Ocean found himself in a tough spot. He was facing charges related to murder and a variety of other offenses. With the possibility of life behind bars, he decided to go rat, becoming a government witness and testifying about a broad range of crimes committed by other DeCavalcante family members in exchange for being granted access to the federal Witness Protection Program.

Vinny admitted to killing Fred Weiss in 1989 as well as to the 1991 murder of Louis "Fat Lou" LaRasso, the old-time DeCavalcante mobster who attended the Apalachin meeting with Nicky Delmore and Frank Majuri way back in 1957. Additionally, he confessed to having participated in planning the hits on gay DeCavalcante capo John D'Amato and, more recently, his own driver and longtime pal

Joseph "Joey O" Masella. Topping it all off, Vinny admitted to the conspiracies to whack Charles "Big Ears" Majuri, DeCavalcante soldier Frank D'Amato, and former Wiggles manager Tom Selvata.

For all of his confessions and information that would lead to charges being brought against a whole bunch of other DeCavalcante guys, Vinny and his family were admitted to the federal Witness Protection Program and relocated to Houston, Texas. While the program is designed to protect participating government witnesses against retaliation from the criminals who they implicate, in the case of Vinny Ocean and some other former DeCavalcante members and associates in witness protection, it doesn't always work out as intended.

Vinny and some other guys in the program have already had their covers blown, making them easily traceable and, thereby, vulnerable to former associates looking to carry out a vendetta hit.

Witness Protection

While being in the program has its benefits for rats, they can still face many challenges in reconciling their new identities and resettling their families.

Anthony Capo, the hit man who pulled the trigger that put gay DeCavalcante capo John D'Amato in an early grave, was one of the guys who took full advantage of the government's offer to become a participating witness and enter "the program."

While witness protection promises to give participants a chance to start a new life under new, assumed identities, there's still a lot it can't protect them from, including old hostilities and grudges held back home. Even when the threats aren't direct, it still must be damaging on a psychological level to know that everyone you grew up with, the guys you worked side by side with for years, all want to see you put out.

When Capo dropped dead at the age of 52 back in 2012, Mafia insiders noted the celebratory mood that rippled throughout goombah circles in New Jersey and New York, one source saying, "There were more people celebrating this on Staten Island than the Giants' win" (Schram, 2012, para. 3). "Once a rat always a rat" is more or less the way things go within the circles of organized crime, and the early death of Capo was no exception. While Capo managed to keep his assumed identity under wraps while in the program, other DeCavalcante guys haven't been so lucky.

Vinny Ocean, due to his high profile and the sheer number of guys he ratted out as a government witness, has had difficulty keeping his new identity a secret. Always the type to make a spectacle of himself—even under the cover of the program—Vinny blew his cover, reverting back to his old business and old ways.

Running a strip club in Houston, Texas, and operating his business out of a gated mansion, it seems that, despite having betrayed his family, little has changed for the former New Jersey-based crook. Living under the moniker James Cabella, Vinny Ocean was outed by the *New York Daily News* in 2009, revealing that local police had been watching the strip club he'd been operating in Houston and suspected that it was a source of drugs and prostitution in the area.

When Vinny Ocean's new identity was exposed, as well as the details of his new business, he had a lot to worry about besides being a potential target. There were many DeCavalcante guys back in his old stomping grounds who wanted him dead, but the media attention on his new Texas-based business being a source of criminal activity in the area was another issue he had to contend with. Choosing to sell his mansion, and presumably split town, Vinny Ocean Palermo, now known as James Cabella, filed for Chapter 11 bankruptcy in 2013. His exact whereabouts today are unconfirmed.

Other books, blogs, and websites that contain writings on the DeCavalcante crime family and their connections to *The Sopranos* have drawn parallels between real-life DeCavalcante boss Vinny Ocean and fictional character Tony Soprano. Citing the facts that they both lived in suburban mansions and owned strip clubs (though true *Sopranos* fans know that Silvio, not Tony, was the on-the-books owner of the Bada Bing), many have suggested that Vinny Ocean was the inspiration behind Tony Soprano.

Here at Mafia Library, we're not going to draw that connection, and here's why: While real-life mobster Vinny Ocean stands as an example of the innate greed that defines some criminals operating within the world of organized crime, true *Sopranos* fans recognize that Tony Soprano, far from being a greed-motivated individual, is a complex character whose motivations, however wavering they may be, are never rooted in the blind pursuit of money or status. Furthermore, Tony becoming a rat just doesn't play with what we understand as his core character traits and motivations. While Vinny Ocean was quick to turn his back on the DeCavalcante family, we can easily and assuredly make the conjecture that Tony would never do the same against the DiMeos.

When asked about any connections between the DeCavalcante family and *The Sopranos*, creator David Chase has pleaded ignorance many times over, suggesting that any overlaps are merely coincidental and repeatedly dropping the anecdote that his mother's house was in the same neighborhood as Genovese mobster Richard "Richie The Boot" Boiardo.

Whether Chase knows more than he's alluding to is up to you, reader, as we've already laid out any connections here as we see them. What is for sure is that around the late 1990s, the DeCavalcante family came under the growing scrutiny of law enforcement at the same time that HBO's *The Sopranos* began airing, leading to an interesting confluence between the worlds of real-life crime and entertainment pop culture.

CHAPTER 9
THE REAL SOPRANOS

At the cusp of the millennium, in the late 1990s, New York City found itself at an inflection point. While there was a push toward sanitization and "Disneyfication" of the streets of New York under the leadership of Mayor Rudy Giuliani, things over in New Jersey remained in many ways the same as they ever were. But over time, the winds of change began to drift in, though they still mingled with the putrid odors that wafted into Jersey across the Goethals Bridge from Staten Island's Fresh Kills Landfill.

That particular landfill in Western Staten Island was yet to become the site of the massive forensics investigation of debris from the collapsed Twin Towers of the World Trade Center. After terrorists flew 2 Boeing 767s into the towers on September 11, 2001, the area was forever changed, leaving a deep gash throughout lower Manhattan and the whole New York area, both physically and psychologically.

When Ralphie Guarino carried out his bank heist at the World Trade Center, it was at a time when the city was grappling with the lingering effects of the crack epidemic, and the elevated crime rates brought with it, but was also enjoying a time of prosperity previously unseen. As the dotcom boom compelled Wall Street to pile in on what became a jaw-dropping 400% rise in the NASDAQ index between 1995 and 2000 ("Dot-com Bubble," 2023), it seemed like there was no limit to how far the financial markets and the city itself could climb.

When Giuliani came in as mayor in 1994, he promised to clean up the streets and restore a sense of safety and security to the city, and in many ways, he delivered on that promise. But, he'll forever be remembered for his roundups of homeless people and his staunch support of broken-windows policing, and even his endorsement of outright police brutality.

It was through this embrace of violent crackdowns that this era also came to be defined by social and political unrest as much as by the efforts to clean up the streets. Protests erupted in response to the unjustified killing of Amadou Diallo at the hands of the NYPD, and tensions between the police and communities of color were boiling over. The streets were lit up with anger and frustration as people marched and rallied to demand justice and accountability from law enforcement.

While local police precincts focused on cleaning up quality-of-life issues that were affecting many of the White gentrifiers who were starting to move into "rough" areas across Manhattan and the outer boroughs, the Feds were working on clean-up campaigns of their own—trying to destabilize local LCN Mafia organizations, including, of course, the DeCavalcante family.

Amid all of this, the TV show *The Sopranos* premiered, becoming an instant hit and a cultural phenomenon. The show was set in New Jersey and was loosely based on the real-life activities of the same real-life local crime families that the Feds were after. As the show gained popularity, the lines between TV and reality began to blur, audiences and wiseguys alike becoming fans.

As would be later revealed in courtroom testimony, the real-life mobsters were very much aware of the portrayals of characters like them in popular culture, largely driven by the popularity of *The Sopranos*. Reflecting their own traits and cultural references back onto themselves in a way that differed from previous portrayals of mob life, *The Sopranos* represented a truly new form of Mafia pop culture and entertainment.

Whether or not David Chase had any particular inspiration from real-life mob families isn't core to the success of the show. What made *The Sopranos* different from other Mafia-related movies and TV shows that came before it was that it delved into the domestic lives and interior realities faced by mobsters in a novel, modern way. Not everything was about "the life": It became about the inner lives, the motivations, the dream realms, and the psychology of *being* a made guy in a Mafia family. It's for this reason why *The Sopranos* remains a fan favorite today—and why the real stories of Mafia families like the DeCavalcante family can only be told in a concise, more modern way that focuses on the personalities behind the stories.

CONCLUSION

While some Mafia books read like a shuffled-up Rolodex of monikers and a muddy recounting of who-whacked-who narratives that leave readers scratching their heads—or, worse yet, lead them to put the book down—we here at Mafia Library are committed to offering you, the reader, the best and most well-organized histories of real-life Mafia families. If you enjoyed this book, don't forget to leave a positive rating, and if you didn't, well… let's just say we got friends who got other friends, and uh, they're gonna stop by and take you for a ride…

REFERENCES

Amoruso, D. (2015, August 21). *Profile of DeCavalcante crime family capo Charles Stango*. Gangsters Inc. https://gangstersinc.org/profiles/blogs/profile-of-decavalcante-crime-family-capo-charles-stango

Anastasia, G. (2010, July 6). *Large living, small income key in Perna mob case*. TMCnet. https://www.tmcnet.com//usubmit/2010/07/06/4885460.htm (Republished from *The Philadelphia Inquirer*)

Anthony Capo. (2022, September 5). In *Wikipedia*. https://en.wikipedia.org/w/index.php?title=Anthony_Capo&oldid=1108593767

Anthony Rotondo. (2021, September 16). In *Wikipedia*. https://en.wikipedia.org/w/index.php?title=Anthony_Rotondo&oldid=1044712717

Apalachin meeting. (2023, January 11). In *Wikipedia*. https://en.wikipedia.org/w/index.php?title=Apalachin_meeting&oldid=1132954702

ARIIA2020. (2021, November 24). *Charles "Big Ears" Majuri is the son of former consigliere Frank Majuri. Upon Giacomo Amari's death, John Riggi appointed Majuri* [Online forum post]. Reddit.

https://www.reddit.com/r/CosaNostra/comments/r1nzqw/charles_big_ears_majuri_is_the_son_of_former/

Associated Press. (2007, September 10). Rudy's love/hate relationship with the mob. *CBS News*. https://www.cbsnews.com/news/rudys-love-hate-relationship-with-the-mob/

Associated Press. (2015, March 12). FBI announces 10 New Jersey Mafia arrests. *Courier-Post*. http://www.courierpostonline.com/story/news/crime/2015/03/12/fbi-announces-new-jersey-mafia-arrests/70211880/

The Blade [Toledo, Ohio]. (1960, November 29). 20 Apalachin convictions ruled invalid on appeal. A1.

Brean, H. (2008, November 2). Charges dropped, but ex-mob hit suspect can't get work card. *Las Vegas Review-Journal*. https://www.reviewjournal.com/news/charges-dropped-but-ex-mob-hit-suspect-cant-get-work-card/

bryson3. (n.d.). *The Philadelphia mob wars*. Timetoast Timelines. Retrieved February 4, 2023, from https://www.timetoast.com/timelines/mob-war-1980-s-2000-s

Burns, F. A. (1991, March 8). Prosecutors: Scarfo running mob from federal prison cell. *UPI*. https://www.upi.com/Archives/1991/03/08/Prosecutors-Scarfo-running-mob-from-federal-prison-cell/5769668408400/

Call 2 alleged mafia kingpins to Trenton. (1967, December 7). *The Paterson News*, 53.

Capeci, J. (2005). *The complete idiot's guide to the Mafia* (p. 366). Alpha Books.

Cascio, J. (2022, September 16). *Stefano Badami (1888–1955)*. WikiTree. Retrieved February 4, 2023, from https://www.wikitree.com/wiki/Badami-183

Castronovo Fusco, M. A. (1999, October 10). City life; How a church brings life to Newark's Little Italy. *The New York Times*. https://www.nytimes.com/1999/10/10/nyregion/city-life-how-a-church-brings-life-to-newark-s-little-italy.html

Commission of Investigation. (2004). *The changing face of organized crime in New Jersey: A status report*. State of New Jersey. https://www.state.nj.us/sci/pdf/ocreport.pdf

Daily News Editorial Board. (2022, December 12). Keeping the mob off the waterfront: U.S. Supreme Court should stop New Jersey from killing docks watchdog. *New York Daily News*. https://www.nydailynews.com/opinion/ny-edit-waterfront-commission-organized-crime-20221212-yxxk45rnyrgdxkcp3z4eozvy54-story.html

Daly, M. (2017, July 11). Jersey's true-life Tony Soprano: Meet the DeCavalcante crime family. *The Daily Beast*. https://www.thedailybeast.com/jerseys-true-life-tony-soprano-meet-the-decavalcante-crime-family

DeCavalcante crime family. (2022, December 26). In *Wikipedia*. https://en.wikipedia.org/w/index.php?title=DeCavalcante_crime_family&oldid=1129651952

DeCavalcante family. (2022, November 23). Button Guys: The New York Mafia. https://thenewyorkmafia.com/decavalcante-family/

DeCavalcante family re-induction ceremonies (1988). (2018, January 26). *LCN Bios*. https://lcnbios.blogspot.com/2018/01/decavalcante-family-re-induction.html

Deseret News. (1990, December 20). U.S. says mob controls casino workers' union. https://www.deseret.com/1990/12/20/18897069/u-s-says-mob-controls-casino-workers-union

Dickson, M. (2018, September 10). *DeCavalcante family*. American Mafia History. https://americanmafiahistory.com/decavalcante-family/

Dot-com bubble. (2023, January 30). In *Wikipedia*. https://en.wikipedia.org/w/index.php?title=Dot-com_bubble&oldid=1136434848

Epstein, S. (2010, August 4). Reputed head of mob crime family, N.J. man are indicted on extortion charges. *NJ.com*. https://www.nj.com/news/2010/08/head_of_mob_crime_family_nj_ma.html

Farrell, B., & Capeci, J. (1988, January 6). Hit, informer linked: Feds think victim let a fink into the mob. *New York Daily News*, 14. https://nydailynews.newspapers.com/clip/85708455/vincent-rotondo-hit-decavalcante/

The FBI Files. (2021, October 16). *The great Philly mob war | FULL EPISODE* [Video]. YouTube. https://www.youtube.com/watch?v=ZcCyu47auWM

Feds nab 120 for fraud. (2000, June 14). *CNN.* https://money.cnn.com/2000/06/14/companies/fraud/

Ford, A. (2019, September 29). Mob NJ: The Mafia is still here, tied to Port Newark and the suburbs. *Asbury Park Press.* https://www.app.com/story/news/investigations/2019/03/28/nj-mob-the-mafia-is-still-here-port-newark-suburbs/3268727002/

Francesco Guarraci. (2021, February 17). In *Wikipedia.* https://en.wikipedia.org/w/index.php?title=Francesco_Guarraci&oldid=1007258050

Gangsters Inc. (2010, November 10). *Turncoat mobster once again involved in dirty business.* https://gangstersinc.org/profiles/blogs/turncoat-mobster-once-again

Gangsters Inc. (2011, November 7). Nicky Scarfo Junior following in daddy's footsteps. https://gangstersinc.org/profiles/blogs/nicky-scarfo-junior-following-in-daddy-s-footsteps

Gangsters: The Documentaries. (2021, September 27). *The real Sopranos: The DeCavalcante crime family (a history)* [Video]. YouTube. https://www.youtube.com/watch?v=POugXFJyA_U&t=12s

Garrett T. (2009, March 26). *The DeCavalcante crime family* [Online forum post]. Organized Crime Rpg.

https://organizedcrimerpg.board-directory.net/t20-the-decavalante-crime-family

Grutzner, C. (1970, January 24). Mafia obtained secret U.S. data. *The New York Times*. https://www.nytimes.com/1970/01/24/archives/mafia-obtained-secret-us-data-tapes-show-they-knew-of-fbi-charts-on.html

Hamilton, B. (2021, July 17). Bringing down "The Sopranos" for the FBI destroyed my life. *New York Post*. https://nypost.com/2021/07/17/bringing-down-the-sopranos-for-the-fbi-destroyed-my-life/

Heneage, B. (2002, March 23). *Sam Monaco*. Find a Grave. Retrieved February 4, 2023, from https://www.findagrave.com/memorial/6284744/sam-monaco

Holguin, J. (2003, May 1). Mob boss 'hit' over gay encounters. *CBS News*. https://www.cbsnews.com/news/mob-boss-hit-over-gay-encounters/

Horowitz, B. (2016, January 7). 3 top Lucchese crime family members sentenced in gambling case. *NJ.com*. https://www.nj.com/morris/2016/01/3_lucchese_crime_family_members_sentenced_in_massi.html

Hunt, T.P. (n.d.-a). *Organized crime's presence in Pennsylvania, 1970*. The American Mafia. https://mafiahistory.us/maf-pcc70.html

Hunt, T.P. (n.d.-b). *Philadelphia mob leaders*. The American Mafia. https://mafiahistory.us/maf-b-ph.html

icegoodbarbPresident. (2008, March 28). *New Jersey Mafia comeback* [Online forum post]. StreetGangs.com. http://www.streetgangs.com/billboard/viewtopic.php?t=40416

In plain sight: Mob brutality on the streets of New York. (2022, December 14). *New York Daily News.* https://www.nydailynews.com/new-york/nyc-crime/plain-sight-gallery-1.14260

Johnson, T. (2016, May 26). Mob still a problem in New Jersey's waste management sector. *WHYY.* https://whyy.org/articles/mob-still-a-problem-in-new-jerseys-waste-management-sector/

Joseph Miranda. (2022, March 4). In *Wikipedia.* https://en.wikipedia.org/w/index.php?title=Joseph_Miranda&oldid=1075127854

Katz, W. (2001). Sticking together, falling apart: "The Sopranos" and the American moral order. *New Labor Forum, 9,* 91–99. https://www.jstor.org/stable/40342317

Kocieniewski, D. (1999, January 17). Decline and fall of an empire. *The New York Times.* https://www.nytimes.com/1999/01/17/nyregion/decline-and-fall-of-an-empire.html

Larsen, E. (2021, April 9). Reputed mob associate from Toms River sentenced to 15 months in federal prison. *Asbury Park Press.* https://www.app.com/story/news/local/courts/2021/04/09/reputed-mob-associate-toms-river-sentenced-15-months-federal-prison/7163859002/

Lee, J. C. (2016, October 12). From Sabella to Merlino: Five Philadelphia mob bosses who impacted Pennsylvania and New Jersey. *PennLive*. https://www.pennlive.com/life/2016/10/philadelphia_mob_boss_crime.html

Lehmann, J. (2002, June 21). Feds' bust rips cover off '89 "hit." *New York Post*. https://nypost.com/2002/06/21/feds-bust-rips-cover-off-89-hit/

Lehmann, J. (2003a, May 8). "Family" favorite—Jersey mobster: They based "The Sopranos" on us. *New York Post*. https://nypost.com/2003/05/08/family-favorite-jersey-mobster-they-based-the-sopranos-on-us/

Lehmann, J. (2003b, May 16). Hunting for the "Beast." *New York Post*. https://nypost.com/2003/05/16/hunting-for-the-beast/

Lehmann, J. (2003c, May 1). Mobster sleeps with the swishes. *New York Post*. https://nypost.com/2003/05/01/mobster-sleeps-with-the-swishes/

Little, B. (2022, February 9). What's it really like in the federal witness protection program? *A&E*. https://www.aetv.com/real-crime/whats-it-really-like-in-witness-protection

Maggio, J. (Executive Producer, Producer/Director, & Writer). (2015, February 7). La Famiglia (Episode 1) [TV docuseries episode]. In *The Italian Americans*. PBS.

Martin, M. (2000, June 15). 120 charged, with promise of more to come: U.S. busts stock scam with ties to the mob. *The New York Times*. https://www.nytimes.com/2000/06/15/news/120-charged-with-promise-of-more-to-come-us-busts-stock-scam-with-ties.html

Milner, B. (2000, June 15). Mob members arrested in securities fraud sweep. *The Globe and Mail.* https://www.theglobeandmail.com/report-on-business/mob-members-arrested-in-securities-fraud-sweep/article18423672/

The Mob Museum. (2019, May 29). *Rudolph Giuliani.* https://themobmuseum.org/notable_names/rudolph-giuliani/

The mob was the city's watchdog during Giuliani cleanup. (n.d.) In *Encyclopedia.com.* Retrieved January 20, 2023, from https://www.encyclopedia.com/law/educational-magazines/mob-was-citys-watchdog-during-giuliani-cleanup

New Jersey Italian and Italian American Heritage Commission. (2010). *Italian Immigration to New Jersey, 1890.* https://www.njitalianheritage.org/wp-content/uploads/2015/12/Italian-Immigration-to-New-Jersey-1890.pdf

The New York Times. (1971, March 16). Five years given to DeCavalcante. https://www.nytimes.com/1971/03/16/archives/five-years-given-to-decavalcante-bid-to-change-gaming-plea-to-not.html

Origins of the St. Rocco Feast. (2008). *Around About Peterstown,* (59), 1. https://www.rennamedia.com/wp-content/uploads/2016/11/aapaug08.pdf

Philadelphia crime family. (2023, January 20). In *Wikipedia*. https://en.wikipedia.org/w/index.php?title=Philadelphia_crime_family&oldid=1134736817

Philip Abramo. (2022, December 25). In *Wikipedia*. https://en.wikipedia.org/w/index.php?title=Philip_Abramo&oldid=1129490842

Pillets, J. (2017, March 22). SCI: Illegal dirt dumpers posing as recyclers. *northjersey.com*. https://www.northjersey.com/story/news/watchdog/2017/03/22/sci-illegal-dirt-dumpers-posing-recyclers/99498420/

The Press of Atlantic City. (2015, September 25). Friday, March 8, 1991 - Scarfo 37 others indicted / state alleges racketeering. https://pressofatlanticcity.com/friday-march-8-1991---scarfo-37-others-indicted-state-alleges-racketeering/article_f0f3447c-5f83-11df-802d-001cc4c03286.html

Pump and dump. (2021, July 7). In *The Sopranos Wiki*. https://sopranos.fandom.com/wiki/Pump_and_dump?oldid=15360

Rashbaum, W. K. (1988, January 5). Feds were investigating slain union organizer. *UPI*. https://www.upi.com/Archives/1988/01/05/Feds-were-investigating-slain-union-organizer/7660568357200/

Ribera Club Celebrates 85th Year With Grand Opening of Cultural Center. (2008). *Around About Peterstown*, (59), 20. https://www.rennamedia.com/wp-content/uploads/2016/11/aapaug08.pdf.

Roberts, S. (2015, August 13). John Riggi, who led New Jersey crime family, dies at 90. *The New York Times.* https://www.nytimes.com/2015/08/12/nyregion/john-riggi-former-head-of-decavalcante-crime-family-dies-at-90.html

Rocco, G., & Schofield, D. (2021). *Giovanni's Ring.* Chicago Review Press.

Rotondo crew (1977–2001). (2018, January 27). *LCN Bios.* https://lcnbios.blogspot.com/2018/01/rotondo-crew-1977-2001.html

Santolo, D. (2016, January 7). *Lucchese crime family mobsters sentenced in massive gambling operation.* About the Mafia. https://aboutthemafia.com/lucchese-crime-family-mobsters-sentenced-in-massive-gambling-operation/

Scarpo, E. (2014, November 5). DeCavalcante redux: NJ family a force to be reckoned with. *Cosa Nostra News.* https://www.cosanostranews.com/2014/11/decavalcante-redux-nj-family-force-to.html

Scarpo, E. (2016, August 24). Sopranos based on which crime family? Not DeCavalcantes... *Cosa Nostra News.* https://www.cosanostranews.com/2016/08/sopranos-based-on-which-crime-family.html

Schram, J. (2012, January 25). Mob rat squeals no more. *New York Post.* https://nypost.com/2012/01/25/mob-rat-squeals-no-more/

Sheehy, K. (2020, June 30). Alleged mobster in Dina Manzo case is real NJ "family" guy, feds say. *Page Six.*

https://pagesix.com/2020/06/30/alleged-mobster-in-dina-manzo-case-is-real-nj-family-guy-feds/

Silver, C. (2022, September 3). *How the nation's most powerful crime boss faked insanity for decades to avoid prison*. All That's Interesting. https://allthatsinteresting.com/vincent-gigante

Smith, G. B. (2003). *Made Men*. Penguin.

South, T. (2016, December 7). Mob captain for gang that inspired "The Sopranos" admits to murder plot. *northjersey.com*. https://www.northjersey.com/story/news/crime/2016/12/07/mob-captain-gang-inspired-sopranos-admits-murder-plot/95101678/

St. James, E. (2011, April 13). *The Sopranos: "Christopher."* The A.V. Club. https://www.avclub.com/the-sopranos-christopher-1798167916

Staff. (2003, November 16). DeCavalcante power structure [Infographic]. *Asbury Park Press*, A4.

Star-Ledger Editorial Board. (2019, July 7). Anti-Sopranos bill will stop the mob from dumping toxic debris all over New Jersey. *NJ.com*. https://www.nj.com/opinion/2019/07/anti-sopranos-bill-will-stop-the-mob-from-dumping-toxic-debris-all-over-new-jersey-editorial.html

Stonefelt, E. (2021, October 20). *Philadelphia's own Florida man*. Mafia Bloodlines: A Society Unto Themselves. https://mafia.substack.com/p/philadelphias-own-florida-man

Tarrazi, A. (2017, April 4). 2 Union County DeCavalcante crime family members admit selling cocaine. *Patch*.

https://patch.com/new-jersey/westfield/2-union-county-decavalcante-crime-family-members-admit-selling-cocaine

thisblogofours. (2013, January 2). *DeCavalcante surveillance photos: Part 2: Vinny Ocean and Big Ears Majuri* [Post]. Tumblr. Retrieved February 4, 2023, from https://www.tumblr.com/thisblogofours/39528272175/decavalcante-surveillance-photos-part-2-vinny

Troncone, T. (2006, June 23). *N.J. Mafia family gets new boss.* The Chicago Syndicate. https://www.thechicagosyndicate.com/2006/06/nj-mafia-family-gets-new-boss.html?m=0

U.S. Attorney's Office. (2010, February 18). *Three New Jersey men charged with conspiring to extort the manager of a pizzeria through threat of violence.* Federal Bureau of Investigation. District of New Jersey. https://archives.fbi.gov/archives/newark/press-releases/2010/nk021810b.htm

U.S. Attorney's Office. (2015, August 18). *Ten members and associates of Decavalcante organized crime family arrested.* United States Department of Justice. District of New Jersey. https://www.justice.gov/usao-nj/pr/ten-members-and-associates-decavalcante-organized-crime-family-arrested

U.S. Attorney's Office. (2016, March 30). *Multi-year prison sentences for two New Jersey men who [were] extorting thousands of dollars from Hudson County project.* United States Department of Justice. District of New Jersey. https://www.justice.gov/usao-nj/pr/multi-year-prison-sentences-two-new-jersey-men-who-extorting-thousands-dollars-hudson

U.S. Government Printing Office. (2000, September 3). *Organized crime on Wall Street* (House Hearing, 106 Congress). https://www.govinfo.gov/content/pkg/CHRG-106hhrg67115/html/CHRG-106hhrg67115.htm

United States of America v. Stango (D.N.J. 2015). https://www.scribd.com/document/258592547/DOJ-Criminal-Complaint-DeCavalcante-Family#

Vacari, G. (2021, July 11). *Status of the New Jersey family* [Online forum post]. GangsterBB. http://www.gangsterbb.net/threads/ubbthreads.php?ubb=showthreaded&Number=1015830

Vassar, S. (2021, October 11). Revisiting The Sopranos' Columbus Day episode. *Film School Rejects*. https://filmschoolrejects.com/sopranos-columbus-day-episode/

Vincent Palermo. (2022, December 25). In *Wikipedia*. https://en.wikipedia.org/w/index.php?title=Vincent_Palermo&oldid=1129491102

Vincent "Vinny Ocean" Palermo - The real Tony Soprano. (2023, January 21). Gangsterism Out. https://www.gangsterismout.com/2016/09/vincent-vinny-ocean-palermo-real-tony.html

Vito Spatafore. (2023, January 6). In *The Sopranos Wiki*. https://sopranos.fandom.com/wiki/Vito_Spatafore?oldid=23700

Walsh, J. (2020, November 23). Feds: Philly-South Jersey Mafia targeted 'criminal rackets' in Atlantic City. *Courier Post*. https://www.courierpostonline.com/story/news/2020/11/23/mafia

-la-cosa-nostra-philadelphia-south-jersey-atlantic-city/6392019002/

Where's Johnny? (2022, December 9). In *The Sopranos Wiki*. https://sopranos.fandom.com/wiki/Where%27s_Johnny%3F?oldid=22629

Would a film about the turbulent founding of the DiMeo/Soprano crime family have been a better idea? [Online forum post]. (2019, November 17). Reddit. https://www.reddit.com/r/thesopranos/comments/dxizhq/would_a_film_about_the_turbulent_founding_of_the/

Zambito, T. (2015, March 14). Wiretaps, prison, death take toll on mob family that inspired "The Sopranos," experts say. *NJ.com*. https://www.nj.com/news/2015/03/wiretaps_prison_death_take_toll_on_mob_family_that.html

Milton Keynes UK
Ingram Content Group UK Ltd.
UKHW011558130624
444148UK00005B/76